In Unexpected Places

Death and Dying – Building up a Picture

In Unexpected Places

Death and Dying – Building up a Picture

Ray Brown

BOOKS

Winchester, UK
Washington, USA

First published by O-Books, 2011
O-Books is an imprint of John Hunt Publishing Ltd., The Bothy, Deershot Lodge, Park Lane, Ropley, Hants, SO24 0BE, UK
office1@o-books.net
www.o-books.com

For distributor details and how to order please visit the 'Ordering' section on our website.

ISBN: 978 1 84694 418 5

A CIP catalogue record for this book is available from the British Library.

Design: Stuart Davies

Printed in the UK by CPI Antony Rowe
Printed in the USA by Offset Paperback Mfrs, Inc

CONTENTS

To Pierrette, my wife, without whom I may never have thought of these things.

Introduction

If you start to look for information about death and whatever may follow you will not find a lot. Surprising when you consider that we live in an age when we are literally flooded with information about everything imaginable. If you want to find out about something, check with Google, Wikipedia or others and you will have a wad of information with just a few clicks on your computer. But when you look for information about death which is an event that concerns us all you will not find it easily but scattered in unusual places, in incomplete pieces. You will need to be persistent in your search. If you are determined you will find it among what psychics and spiritualists say, what grief counsellors relate, what myths have told us, what religions have taught. Having found bits and pieces of information the challenge is in seeing how the pieces interrelate, and in seeing which ones match. This book tries to do that. The unexpected places it will look at include age-old African beliefs that tell about life and death, at a Mesopotamian epic that speaks of one man's quest for immortality and how he failed, at ancient Tibetan and Chinese thinking and at the lessons of the world's religions.

Someone[1] once wrote, 'If a man could pass through paradise in a dream and have a flower presented to him as a pledge that he had really been there, and if he found that flower in his hand when he awoke… What then?' But that has never happened and is not likely to happen.

The paradigm most of us live with at the moment is of a short life filled with activity followed by an unknown mystery of indeterminate duration devoid of conceivable activity. We make little attempt to understand all of this, when we do not deny it completely. This book is about how to deal with the puzzle of death more consciously and more comfortably. It is not a book about religion and is not written from any particular religious viewpoint. While it is true that religions have generally tried to explain the mystery of death and afterwards, they have no monopoly of the problems of death and dying. Obviously death is a topic that has been a puzzle for us human beings since our earliest beginnings. This book comes to the conclusion that death, whether our own death or that of someone dear to us, is something that we do not truly confront, at least in the western world. We avoid the topic, avoid trying to understand it in its relationship to life and the living. This book will suggest that we should try to become more aware of death and what it may mean. That this awareness will in fact enrich our lives. Working to increase our awareness of death, that of those dear to us or our own, and our preparedness to face it is something the vast majority of us definitely don't do, apart from taking out some sort of funeral insurance policy to cover expenses. In fact, we act as though thinking or talking about death in any serious way is something morbid. But does the real morbidity not lie there? Is there not an evident case of repression there? Admittedly it is a repression that has become part of our human condition and we have come to accept it as perfectly normal. But is it?

The key lesson that emerges from the explorations in this book is that in order to cross the threshold into death we need to develop selflessness, we need to go beyond individualism. The 'self' is the ego, it is the personality we are attached to and think we know well in our everyday lives: it is what drives us to achieve the things that we believe will satisfy us. We generally find that they don't satisfy us. In the world of death our personality, which is so important to us on earth, has no foothold on that new environment, and it cannot breathe its air. For there us another part of us, the 'Self', as the Orientals have called it, the Soul, which is bigger than the personality and which is impersonal. Death is a different state, obviously, and it is only the Self that can survive happily there.

This book suggests ways by which we can develop that Self so as to make the journey easier.

We live in a world that is full of suffering. Even those of us who live comfortably suffer. And we suffer because there is too much 'self' and not enough 'Self'. Our focus on individualism has done immense damage in our world. It has been the cause of wars, it has created poverty and been at the root of financial and economic disasters. It has created a world in which we are led to be unconscious of the suffering of vast numbers of human beings. And it is responsible for the appalling environmental problems that the planet is likely to face in the coming century.

Thus we have been murderous like Cain. Guilty of the murder of our brothers, guilty of nurturing wars, of causing damage to the environment, of destroying the planet even.

And it has been because we have allowed the self to become too big. We have come to believe we are all-powerful. But this has led only to suffering and disasters.

In this way we can never cope successfully with death. For life and death are intimately interrelated and interdependent. A knowledge of the state of death affects the values we have in our life. As the Vedas say again and again in different words, being able to 'live in death' – live in the Self – is a guarantee of a real life in the world of the living. And can only lead to a better world than the one we now live in.

The ancient Babylonian epic relates the story of Gilgamesh – an object lesson for us even today, and the theme of one of the chapters of this book. A King of Uruk and possessor of everything worldly that he could wish for, Gilgamesh desired immorality and went to great lengths and through many trials to try to achieve it. But in the end he failed, because he could not leave behind his 'self'.

Part One

An Underlying Reality?

Chapter 1

The Storytellers

Another kind of repression?

For most of us a struggle with death as a reality does not exist. It is something we put out of our minds so quickly that we are scarcely conscious of doing that. Most of us, I think, live with the notion that death is not an immediate concern of ours, or at least in no future near enough to be worth attention. We are storytellers. For ourselves and for others we invent all kinds of stories and scripts to take our attention off death. We can joke about it and we can sing about it. We can read moving stories and watch moving films about death – other people's deaths. But it's a Scheherazade strategy. Death is an important event for all of us but is there any important event in our lives which receives less attention? We make a fuss about births and marriages, elections, promotions, retirements, the Oscars, war and hurricanes. But we avoid having to talk about death, our own personal encounter with death that is. We avoid having to try to understand it, by telling ourselves stories, by inventing fictions in our lives, by being imaginative. However, while we are imaginative about dying and the pain brought upon us by the loss of those dear to us (remember *Love Story*?), our imagination comes up against serious limits when we have to picture what actually happens to us when we die. And how many of us ever notice that death and dying are around us at every instant of our lives? And it has always been like that. Yet how many have reflected that our earth, as someone once put it,[1] is an earth of cemeteries. There can be no place on earth that did not have a cemetery at some time or other. We live with and on cemeteries. We sleep on cemeteries. We walk on cemeteries. We drive our cars on and through cemeteries. And it has been like that for millions of years. Bones have been piling upon bones all over the earth. And yet death is taboo or at least near-taboo in most of our western societies. Our inevitable encounter with death is something we think about little and talk about less. Fortunately, in a way, our mental constitution grants us this gift for sweeping awkward problems under the carpet, this ready repression. And it's like that for everyone in our societies I think. We go to great lengths to avoid coming face to face with death, and when we do, we go to equally great lengths to quarantine it. We are determined not to turn the spotlight onto it, almost as if we were genetically programmed to avoid looking closely at it. We cover it with a mantle of ceremony and circumstance, music, kind words. We socialize it in other words, we socialize a stranger we know little or nothing about.

There is a triple taboo that enshrouds that better-to-be-avoided topic, death. Not something we like to talk about. Nor something we even like to think about a lot. Not something we feel the need to get ready for, psychologically that is. This may often not be the case for the terminally ill who need to be accompanied in their final days. But do we have to wait to be terminally ill to confront the idea of our death? The only way we can break this triple taboo is by bringing death into our consciousness, by seeing it as necessary in order to understand life, in order to give a meaning to life, just as night gives a meaning to day, winter to summer. And that is one of the main messages we find in incomplete pieces in those unexpected places.

Yet we are all constantly intrigued by the meaning of life. We all have the need to find answers or THE answer. Some of us succeed, or at least find an answer that meets our personal needs. But in trying to understand life many of us leave death out of the equation. 'Out of the equation' in the sense that we do not look upon life and death as complementary. We have night and day, summer and winter, heat and cold etc. And we have life and death. Unconsciously our desire is for life to continue, for death to be denied. We seek permanence in other words. A number of us will say that they accept the idea of death being an end to everything they know. (And, as this book will later hint, they may be right, but not in the way they think.) Yet even the sceptics maybe have an unconscious, tiny little hope that there might be some sort of continuation. These chapters are therefore also an exploration of this desire for permanence. They look at what different cultures have had to say about permanence. What Christians have thought, Buddhists, Moslems, Taoists, Hindus. And many sources that are not religions. All of these sources are found to throw light on the problem of permanence, light from different perspectives perhaps but which reveals a common vision.

But apart from understanding what an afterlife might mean there is the essential fact that people need in some way to be prepared for death whether or not there is an afterlife. After all we prepare for all the other important events in our lives, be it preparing for a wedding, for a job interview, for an athletic event. Perhaps we need to have some clearer notions of the connections between the state of living and the state of... being dead. In the course of this book we will build a picture of what may happen to us after death, after a life on this earth. And the relevance of one of those states to the other. There is no morbidity in this, for morbidity is another pretext we have for avoiding the topic of death: we hate being morbid, especially in front of others.

Later in this book we can see that for many death is not negative and awareness of it should not diminish the joy we have in life. This is not a matter of Faith, though no doubt that is important for many people. It is a question of building, with our powers of judgement and insight, a model that will make sense. In the same way that scientific researchers use the evidence available to form hypotheses which are later confirmed or refuted.

In our everyday lives we spend little or no time thinking of the event, of how we may manage it. We may arrange for others to manage it and in fact the business of making funeral arrangements down to small details of the service is becoming a common phenomenon with new companies handling this sort of thing springing up all the time. In this way all of the practical arrangements for burial or cremation are entrusted to a company and everything neatly paid for in advance. In this way only do we generally prepare for death. The attraction of this is the practical side of it; it doesn't imply a coming face-to-face with death or any attempt to understand it; it is a tacit acceptance of the inevitable and the unknowable. There is nothing here that drives us to refuse the unacceptable. On the contrary there is perhaps something weak in this unquestioning acceptance, an intellectual cowardice, a refusal to explore the Unknowable. Having made our arrangements and signed the contract we continue to distract ourselves with our jobs, our families, our pastimes and other preoccupations. Things that are more important to us. And many of us anyway (most of us?) are hesitant, in company certainly, to approach topics that we feel are very 'serious' like dying. At least we recognize that it is serious! It is true that we can find death paraded before us for our entertainment, in fiction, in TV, film, novels. They allow us to make death an object, something outside us, that we can observe without fear and can even control for we can switch off the film, put down the book, comment on it (death and satire go well together), laugh at it (death and humour also mix well), and feel secure. This is not so with young children who have to learn the difference between fiction and reality and so have to learn to become stronger in the sense that they must become able to control their fear. It is also not true of extremely well-made or well-written films or novels, stories of crimes or war where death can be depicted in a violent but realistic way or in a strongly emotional way. These can destabilize us by stimulating and enhancing the death images that lie deep in our imagination, and so bring us close to feeling the reality of death close at hand. We generally find ourselves attracted and repelled by this confrontation with the unknown and the terrifying. But ultimately we don't follow the path that leads into that darkness, and once the lights go up we classify it as fiction.

But inevitably death as a reality rudely intrudes from time to time and unexpectedly, uninvited, in what may be the otherwise tranquil flow of our lives. Family members die and we are faced with that reality that we had pushed beneath our consciousness, that we believed we were safe from. But even then we have strategies for putting to one side any serious consideration of it. The Irish wake was a very effective strategy. You could enjoy yourself, drink and dance and assure yourself that the departed one was watching you and would be glad to join in. It was as if you were imagining they were not dead at all. You are saying no to death. The undertaker's ministrations, in making the dead presentable, and the interventions of the priest are not attempts to overcome death but to celebrate the life of the deceased and so take our attention away from the EFFECTS of death... Our funeral services are more of a farewell and a celebration of a life than an opportunity to think about and understand better this event. This is perfectly legitimate of course and even necessary but it is only half the story. And to make things more difficult for us, or easier, the funeral parlour nowadays takes death out of our immediate environment; we no longer need to live with the dead body in the house between death and burial or cremation. And while it is true that there are many strong and convincing arguments in favour of cremation, might it not also be true that it can help us achieve closure more quickly? It certainly has nothing to do, in the majority of cases, with the Eastern preference for this method. And probably not many people are aware of the Hindu and Buddhist rule that cremation should not take place before at least three days in order to allow the more spiritual parts of our being to separate themselves from the physical.

As we grow older we become more and more aware of our own mortality. But we develop more and more strategies for avoiding having to confront it.

There are societies that have lived and continue to live closer to death. Gabonese, Nigerian, and other African statues, were figures that allowed people to relate to their ancestors. Aborigines had their ways of communicating with the dead, Amerindian traditions have many examples where the support and advice of the departed is sought. Those peoples made and continue to make themselves familiar with death. They relate to their ancestors, talk to them, listen to them. If we were to do this, and make it known, we are likely to be... well, if not referred to a psychiatrist, at least gently laughed at.

When did we in the west start to be shy of death? There are those who believe it began with the Greeks who of all civilizations were the first to perfectly reproduce the proportions and harmony of natural physical forms. In Greek mythology, for perhaps the first time, death appears as something ominous and sombre – the River Styx, the Underworld. The Greeks, having been able to capture in stone the beauty of physical forms, found themselves suddenly terrified by its transience, by the passing nature of all they could see. All that beauty would disappear, rot even! A thought that filled them with terror, a terror which, though not at the level of our consciousness now, has never really left us. Some have said that it was in order to deal with death that religions arose: to give us hope of some life after it and to allow us to communicate with the departed through prayer. The Day of the Dead, the day after All Saints' Day, was instituted by the Catholic Church to commemorate, mainly, those who had died in the preceding year. It is still taken quite seriously at least by older and more traditional members of the community in Europe who take flowers to the tombs of their families. But it is becoming more and more a minority observance, and not one that is treated very seriously. In some Catholic countries of southern Europe and in central and South America, however, it is still a big festival. And not a morbid one either: it is a celebration of life and of the promise of life after death. In Poland and other central European countries the tradition is to light candles and visit the graves of departed relatives. In some parts of Austria cakes are left for them on the table and the room kept warm for their comfort. Brittany, in north western France, is a place where old traditions die hard. There is still great respect for the dead there and on the Day of the Dead people will go to the cemeteries after night falls to offer holy water on their family graves.

The Chinese day of the dead is in early April or thereabouts in our calendar. The Chinese in China and Taiwan and in all the other countries where there is a diaspora go in their millions to their family graves to take flowers and relate to the dead. I remember when living in Malaysia being advised not to try to go out that day because of the traffic congestion. In the seventh month of the Chinese calendar there is a day when during the night the dead are said to come back and visit the living. The living sit with one another in their houses and, trembling with excitement or fear, wait for unusual noises. I have heard Chinese friends talk about this, not sure in our modern world whether to laugh at it or take it seriously.

In Mexico, in rural areas, for of course the cities are modern, they prepare for the Day of the Dead (*Día de los Muertos*) a long time in advance. They make paper, cardboard and papier-mâché skeletons in homes and schools; give them different names, play with them, dance with them. Children take them to bed. Everyone collects together interesting things to take to the graves which are cleaned and decorated in the days preceding the festival. It's a time of joy. People even dress up as the deceased. They wear bells in their clothes and strings of shells so that as they dance they will wake up the dead. Toys are taken for dead children. Sugar skulls are prepared and sold and eaten. All in an atmosphere of fun: death is not depressing, but the opposite, is the message. The Bon Festival in Japan is over 500 years old and is a Buddhist festival to honour the dead. Families leave the cities and go back to their rural villages where they clean their family tombs and special traditional dances are performed. In all of these cases death is in every way as rich and full as life. Which is not the case in our more developed societies where we are shackled by an embarrassment and awkwardness when we have to handle death.

However, even in our more 'developed' western societies some people, especially widows or widowers, say they continue to talk to their departed partner. This is beautiful and moving but is there not some wishful thinking in it? It's a topic that we can look at more closely in chapter 16. A key point is that it is only due to their bereavement that they come to this: if there is no loss of a loved one, there is no attempt to link with the departed. In the normal course of events people don't try to make any such links. There are of course attempts to contact the dead that are made in séances but these are often dubious and at best may represent contacts with the body that esoteric writers call the 'astral body' or 'astral shell'. This concept of an 'astral body' is not limited to oriental-type séances in western or eastern contexts. The Senoufo people in Mali have ancient traditions and they call this 'astral body' the *nyil*. The *nyil* (see chapter 4, page 38) is distinct from the physical body; it is immaterial and usually not visible to yourself or others; it travels outside the physical body when you sleep, and when you die it disintegrates, though this may take a certain amount of time. It has the form, when you can see it, of the physical body and it has the emotions and thoughts, and will, of the physical body before death.

It is certainly the case that if we reflect for a time on the shortness of our own life, the infinity of space, and the eternity of time before us and after us some explanations would be welcome. And perhaps it is the lack of these explanations that leads to death being a taboo subject. You can't talk about something you know nothing about! Religions, of course, help us deal both with grief and with the welfare in the afterlife of our departed loved ones and so ease the pain inflicted by infinity and eternity. But it could be that this is simplifying the matter, losing sight of some of the issues. Because there is more to it than our grief and our desire that the departed rest in peace. It is true that religions, in their different ways, deal with both death AND life and with how they interact and relate to each other, in the sense that most if not all religions say that how you behave in this life will determine your condition afterwards... But only some religions deal with DYING, how we face and how we help others face the act of dying. And our religions are not especially convincing when they tell us about the kind of existence that may be in store for us after death.

We all at some time or another face the pain of losing a loved one, losing someone for the rest of this life and maybe forever. We ask ourselves where that loved one has gone, we wonder if they continue to exist and in what kind of world. We need help in dealing with this. The next chapter begins by looking at a very old book about death and dying and tries to elucidate what it means for us in practical terms today.

Chapter 2

Beginners

Looking into The Tibetan Book of the Dead (among a few other things)

There is a real sense in which, faced with death, we are all mere beginners. We have had no lessons, no teacher, no book, no course. All through our lives we come regularly face-to-face with death – of friends, family, the famous, and our TV networks feed us daily with accounts of the deaths of the victims of war and of hunger. We are constant witnesses to this 'cessation of activity' that is death. Yet, except for those who are anchored in a Faith we observe and suffer, but cannot explain. Even those who have a Faith go through their periods of blackness and doubt. They too have no proof. So, to the end of our days we go on asking the old question: is there a life after death? What is its nature, its purpose? This problem – that we don't know the answers to these questions, in the usual senses of 'know' – is the reason for our reluctance to face death in a realistic way. What is the nature of the afterlife, if it exists? It can do no harm to begin by looking at what the world's religions have had to say. There have been basically two approaches in the religions of the world. In one approach there is a life after death which takes place in paradise, or in certain cases and for a certain time, in hell, and there may be a period in an intermediary state, which some call 'Purgatory'. But whatever the case there is no return to a normal life on earth. There is one life and one afterlife. The other view is that there are many lives with intervening periods spent in another world, maybe paradise or maybe something else. That is the re-incarnationist point of view best seen in Hinduism and Buddhism. In the first one what you get after death is forever and is a result of your actions in your one life. In the second case life after death still depends on what you do in this life but it is also a preparation for the next life on earth. (Hinduism and Buddhism are not in agreement about what it is that goes from one life to another, but more of that in another chapter.)

Do you have any preferences, between the re-incarnationist view and the one-go view? Most people, unless they are well anchored already in a faith, find it difficult to state a preference; many would even reject both, and find it easier to get back to their daily business and forget about the whole bally thing. It all seems an impossible responsibility and not very relevant to problems that are pressing for decisions that need to be made today, like:

1. how to get promotion in my job
2. what digital camera to buy
3. how to pay less car insurance
4. how to save more money generally
5. what to buy for the kids for Christmas
6. what will it cost to repaint the house

And there are only 24 hours in day to deal with all these things…

Being able to come to terms with death must mean being able to understand its nature. We sometimes talk of our wish to be able 'to understand the meaning of life'. But that may be impossible without at the same time trying to understand the meaning of death. *The Tibetan Book of the Dead,* despite the title, is as much about life as about death. Life and death go together of course and you cannot have one without the other. Death is like the empty spaces between the spokes of a wheel that the Tao talks of: 'We put thirty spokes together and call it a wheel, but it is on the space where there is nothing that the usefulness of the wheel depends.'

The popular quip (that you're a long time dead) may contain

more meaning than is apparent. Human life on Earth is ridiculously short in terms of cosmic time. There are eons before our birth and eternity stretches out after our death. So make the best of it, says the quip. And maybe there is an important lesson there. The origins of The Tibetan Book of the Dead, as is the case with a number of oriental texts, are somewhat obscure. It belongs to the Mahayana School of later Buddhism. Mahayanism is full of a whole world of various beings mostly invisible to us: deities, dakinis, buddhas and bodhisattvas. The Tibetan Book of the Dead was composed by a sage centuries ago and buried in the hills of central Tibet. It was discovered many years later, the legend tells us, and as the sage had planned, by a man called Karma-Lingpa who turned what is in the book into a tradition.

It is a teaching to be given to people who are dying or recently dead. The essential thing to understand is this: the intrinsic characteristics of the state of death are not at all those of our living state. It is something new and unfamiliar. It is like arriving in a land where all the customs are different, and where you don't understand the language and the people. You are unused to their gestures and attitudes and they seem, perhaps mistakenly, strange, hostile and frightening. You feel alone, weak and unprotected and generally sorry for yourself. This is what The Tibetan Book of the Dead calls the *bardo* experience. It happens to us often in our daily lives. We find ourselves in some new situation and feel threatened, insecure, lose our usual confidence, need support. It is the feeling we have when, late at night, we arrive alone in a city we have never visited before, in a country new to us, and one we have come to perhaps through no choice of our own. From our taxi or bus we see the yellow lights of the deserted streets, reflected perhaps in pools of rainwater, each street and square unfamiliar and unsettling. We feel alone, unprotected, nostalgic for what we have left behind: family, friends, familiar places and routines. The Tibetan Book of the Dead explains to the dying that this is what they will meet after death and prepares them for it. It tells them in considerable detail that they will experience certain visions, see lights, some intensely, unbearably bright and some soft and inviting. When we are confronted with things totally new and unfamiliar we will always try to interpret them in terms that we can handle. In the new environment which we enter after death therefore the Christian will see things in terms of heaven and angels, hell and demons, the Virgin Mary, Jesus; the Moslem in terms of the gardens and springs, houris with large eyes as companions and other delights of paradise, or in the case of a sinner the fires of Hell. And in the culture of the Tibetan Book of the Dead post-death phenomena will be interpreted in the terms of Mahayana Buddhism. The dying person is also told that he or she will see visions that may appear terrifying but that they should not be afraid as the visions come from within their own minds. Those that are most frightening come around the tenth day after death (to those, probably most of us, who haven't been able to attain enlightenment in the preceding days). At this point visions of Gods and Goddesses appear before the dead person, dancing with skulls of blood in their hands, swinging crescent knives and playing instruments made with human bones and skin. During the first six days, however, each day brings a vision of a particular deity with a generally benevolent nature. Each has a dominant colour and the visions are surrounded by lights of varying degrees of intensity. On the first day after death (actually the first day after several days' unconsciousness) the dominant colour of the light is blue, on the second, white, on the third, yellow, on the fourth red and on the fifth green. In all cases the dead person is told to try to go for the unbearably bright light, rather than towards the soft, comfortable lights.

These visions are derived from the particular culture of Tibetan tantric Buddhism and seem outlandish to people from another culture. But perhaps the important point is to see the concepts behind the deities who appear each day to the dead person. The first deity to appear on the first day is Vairocana who represents endless space. The dead person finds himself/herself in infinity, and at one and the same time everywhere in infinity. You have no idea of front or back or of centre or periphery, you are both centre and periphery. It is 'limitless, all-pervading space in which everything exists as it really is'. This is the opportunity to emerge from ignorance into wisdom, from confusion to clarity. The second day brings the deity Akshobya who represents aggression and hatred with their antidote, a 'mirror-like wisdom, which reflects everything calmly and uncritically'. The third day is the turn of Ratnasambhava who personifies pride, the antidote to which is the wisdom of equality and equanimity. The fourth day is Amitabha who symbolises passion and desire; the antidote to these is discrimination 'which provides the coolness and detachment for passion to be transformed into compassion'. And the fifth day is reserved for Amoghasiddhi who symbolizes karma[1] and action and finding the ability to counteract hindrances that may prevent us from performing good actions. The principal of these karmic hindrances is envy (and the colour associated with Amoghasiddhi is green!). The solution is a wisdom which impregnates all actions, taking no sides, and seeing love and hate, for example, as one. Despite the exoticism and colourfulness of these representations they represent certain constants of the human condition: ignorance, aggression, pride, passion, envy. Perhaps these representations are asking us some important questions about our lives, are in fact giving us five tests:

1. How did we deal with ignorance when confronted with it, our own or in others?
2. How did we deal with aggression and hatred, in our selves and when directed against us?
3. How did we deal with pride?

4. How did we deal with passion and desire?
5. How did we manage envy, our own or in response to the envy of others? Did we allow wisdom to govern our actions?

These are after all five defects that if not managed well can ruin us as human beings. I think it is important to remark at this point upon something that will come back again and again in later chapters. In order to observe and reflect on these feelings we need to have some kind of consciousness after death. How similar is this to the consciousness we have while alive, which, we would have to admit, is often inattentive, unobservant and unfocused?

There are similarities in all this with what we find in modern day psychology. The terrifying visions come from within us, from our unconscious: a reflection of our life's inner struggles in the face of our less-than-admirable actions and thoughts? And accepting aggression and hatred 'calmly and uncritically' like a mirror, controlling passion through 'discrimination', and so changing passion into compassion, have also surely a modern ring. The Tibetan Book of the Dead focuses on five human weaknesses and states them in a negative form. The last four can be found in the other major religions without difficulty. And even the problem of 'ignorance' is in them, explicitly in the Koran and also though less explicitly in Christianity. Jesus Christ gives the example of the five foolish virgins who didn't foresee the oil they needed, in other words that they didn't know they had to prepare themselves for the realization of the Self – the coming of the Holy Spirit in Christian terms. They were not clear about who they were and what they were supposed to do.

While these 'constants of the human condition' are also central to the other religions, in The Tibetan Book of the Dead we are told how we can observe them after death, their natures and their antidotes. There is a parallel here to the Day of Judgement and to the Angel holding the book, in Christianity, or, in Islam, to the angel who bears witness to the deeds of the recently deceased person. The difference is that in the Buddhist version the purpose is pedagogy and not inflicting some sort of penalty or reward.

The Tibetan Book of the Dead, then, is a handbook about how to manage one's death, and how to help others pass through it. In particular how to recognize that the events that follow it are an opportunity to learn, are pedagogic that is, not reward or punishment. It is fundamentally based on the assumption that death is a passing from one kind of reality into another and that people are not prepared for that second kind of reality and most probably will not understand it without some sort of briefing. Despite the cultural differences there is something practical about this; it seems to resemble the kind of thing we need if we are to be more knowledgeable and prepared for death. There is in it something that seems to be dynamic and interactive. This picture of death isn't static and motionless, there is movement in it.

It is worthwhile noting that in what are often considered to be very primitive beliefs, these same preoccupations are present. African secret initiatic societies, for example, taught the initiate that death and life are interconnected, that death is the flip-side of life and vice-versa. To take one example, in an initiatic society in Mali in West Africa the young initiate, for a whole night, is buried up to his neck in soft earth, mixed with decaying carcass. From then on he should never fear the smell of decaying flesh and he will understand that death is part of life. The same society taught that death is in fact a birth into a new life and that coming back to earth is a death to a higher life.

Some would see these ideas as being more useful than the ideas that we find of heaven and hell in Christianity and in Islam. Of course we should bear in mind that there is a difference between what we can call 'popular belief' and a more esoteric interpretation. In twelfth century Spain, in the Caliphate of Cordoba, there was a Moslem philosopher called Averroes, Abdul-Wahid Ibn Rushd by his Arabic name, who tackled the question of popular beliefs versus philosophical interpretation. He states that 'The reality of resurrection is a matter about which all religions are in agreement'. But he admits that the exact nature of the soul and the afterlife are more difficult to describe. He spends time reflecting on whether the afterlife is really such as it is described in the Koran and concludes that the language of the Holy Book, the beautiful gardens, damsels and fine wines, are a way of expressing in familiar terms things that we cannot comprehend. 'Religions have differed as regards the states of the happy or miserable souls after death. Some do not speak of them because they are spiritual states not physical. Those who depict the physical pleasures of the afterlife do not mention any harm that might be associated with them.' For, when we reflect on it, some of the things we might enjoy in paradise could be dangerous for the health.

But Averroes thinks that it is better to leave the masses of the public in their simple beliefs, otherwise 'religion will be torn apart'. As for other people 'the truth of the matter is that it is incumbent on each person to take the position to which his speculation leads him; provided such speculation does not lead to the denial of existence after death', which would make him an unbeliever. Regarding the detail of the nature of life after death, Averroes concludes that to believe that we have a physical body is absurd, and ends up suggesting that the kind of body we have in the afterlife is different from that of our present life.

As for the environment we find ourselves in after death, we can find that the literal, popular interpretations of the Koran (the springs of pure water, the gardens, the *houris*) exist, in a slightly different form, in the writings of esoteric Buddhism. For it is said there that after a certain period in a state they call *kama loca* the departed soul moves to a state called *devachan* and in this state he or she enjoys to the full what gave the most emotional pleasure in life especially those things that carry a moral and aesthetic mark. A Buddhist writer put it in the following way:

> The purely sensual feelings and tastes of the late personality will drop off from it in devachan, but it does not follow that nothing is perceivable in that state except feelings and thoughts having a direct relevance to religion and spiritual philosophy. On the contrary, all the superior phases, even of sensuous emotion, find their appropriate sphere of development in Devachan.

A kind of Paradise, in short. But looking at it more closely this state of *devachan* turns out to be a dream-state, born of our imagination (see page 26 below).

The Resurrection of the body is central to Christianity and, if you take a very strict orthodox view, that resurrection is of the physical body as we know it. And, most believers would assume, with the personal identity we have had in this life, though this is stated in no place. If we base ourselves on the Gospels, and look at the event which was the Resurrection of Jesus Christ, we have two things:

1. The physical body in the Tomb disappeared completely
2. Disciples on more than one occasion encountered Jesus after death in a physical body.

Well, 'in a physical body'... Matthew and Mark don't actually say that, in fact Mark at one point says he appears 'in another form' to two of the disciples. In the Gospel of Luke, on the road to Emmaus, two disciples did not recognize Jesus, taking him for a stranger. In the Gospel of John also Jesus appeared to his disciples by the Lake Tiberias but they 'knew not that it was Jesus'. The sheer paucity of information about the exact nature of this resurrected body and the problems of identification must alert us to the fact that there is more here than meets the eye. If we look at the Gnostic Gospels we find there is little mention of resurrection. It would look as if there was a great deal of disagreement and a general lack of clarity among the early Christians as to what this resurrection actually meant. Was it in the physical body? Was only the soul eternal? Was there reincarnation? Was there retention of the personal identity? Does consciousness survive? There is a Gnostic document called the Treatise on the Resurrection, dated between 170 and 200 of our era, which tries to explain Resurrection in logical terms. In words, however, that do not seem to be chosen for their clarity, the writer describes the resurrection of Jesus by saying he 'swallowed the visible by the invisible'. He talks of the 'spiritual resurrection which swallows up the psychic in the same way as the fleshly'. This would seem to imply that those particular early Christians saw the resurrection as not being in any physical body. But not only that for if it 'swallows up the psychic' it goes beyond the mind, the ordinary consciousness, the personality. In the resurrection, the treatise says, you find what you lack; this world is perishable, impermanent, corrupted, subject to constant change. So whatever 'body' we have in resurrection is something permanent. The 'visible members' (of our body) do not survive death, it says, but 'the living members which exist within them' will rise. 'Living' here must mean something more than physically living. The resurrection is leaving the world of change and impermanence for a world of permanence. The writer is very clear that the resurrection will not be in the flesh. 'So never doubt concerning the resurrection! For if you were not existing in flesh, you received flesh when you entered this world. Why will you not receive flesh when you enter the Aeon? That which is better than flesh is that which is (for) the cause of life.' The world is an illusion, the Treatise tells us, not the resurrection.

It is generally said that it is the 'soul' which survives death.

The exact nature of what we call the soul has always eluded description. But that should not be surprising. It is the Self of the Vedas and the other Hindu scriptures, it is the 'individuality of Buddhism,[2] the God Within of Christianity. Averroes wrote of the soul: 'The scripture does not expressly disclose to the public what the soul is. The Precious Book says: "And [if] they ask you about the spirit, say, 'The spirit is in my Lord's command and you have not been given except a little knowledge.'"'

In the Koran it is said: 'If the sea was ink for you to write the words of my Lord, the sea would be dry before the words of the Lord were put down even if you were to bring a quantity of water equal to the first.'

The Buddha also, it is said, while one day in a forest with his disciples, was asked about the nature of God. He is said to have taken in his hand from the forest floor a handful of dry leaves and to have said: 'What you see in my hand is what I can teach you in this life. What there is to know is like all the leaves in this forest.'

The notion of 'soul' has also to be described differently depending on whether you take a re-incarnationist view or not. In the one-life religions (Christianity, Judaism, Islam) we can see that it is already difficult to have a clear idea what constitutes the soul. In the religions where there is reincarnation (Hinduism, Buddhism) the situation is more complicated for whatever the soul is, it moves from one life to another. If a Christian or Moslem or Jew takes the trouble to cross to the other side of the mirror and put themselves in the shoes of an Oriental, a Buddhist or a Hindu, and look back at their own religion, they would find it very strange that there could be a very short life in the physical body followed by an eternity after it, and even stranger that the nature of that eternity, heaven or hell, is determined by the acts in one short life on earth despite the great differences of conditions, rich or poor, healthy, sickly, into which people are born. As a Buddhist or Hindu you would accept as natural that the conditions into which you are born in this life, and the handicaps you may have to face, physical, intellectual or material, are the result of what you did in your past lives. And so the concept of a 'soul' has got to be extended in time, over a succession of lives. But it is still not clear what constitutes the soul: does it have personality and consciousness, for example? Successive lives, from the standpoint of reincarnation, are like the classes that children go through in school, steps on the road to becoming more fulfilled. In the case of a school it is the same child, getting older and more mature of course, who goes through the classes. But what changes and what remains the same from one incarnation to the other?

In Hindu and Buddhist thinking the period between death and rebirth can be very long indeed. This is a period of living the EFFECTS of the previous life on earth (the world of CAUSES). After death there is period called *kama loca* which is close to our physical life and during which the more earthly elements of our psyche are slowly discarded leaving us with the more spiritual and purer elements that were with us in life. During this period perceiving the living, seeing them, hearing them, is possible but communication rare. The period of *kama loca* can be very long and the dead person gradually 'forgets' his or her past life or at least the small details of it, in the same way as someone who has moved to a totally new country and spent some years there loses contact with those he or she left behind and the memories of the old country become vague and less important and not relevant. Then, as already mentioned, the soul enters the realm the Hindus call *devachan*. In many ways this is the equivalent of the Christian heaven, or the Moslem paradise. In general and for most people it is a period when they enjoy a state of happiness reliving the happiest moments of their lives, with the ones they loved and were close to on earth, and engaging in the activities they used to enjoy. (This is reminiscent of the frescoes on the walls of the Pharaohs' tombs which depict hunting and fishing and making merry, the things the Pharaohs enjoyed about life.) BUT it is an entirely subjective world, the world of *devachan*. However, when you think about it, it is no more subjective than the world in which we live in our lives on earth which is itself full of illusion. After all, though we have the illusion that we are standing still, we are actually hurtling through space at great speed. And while we think of ourselves as a solid body we are in reality a mass of atoms with great spaces between them. All the pleasurable activities and interactions we may enjoy in *devachan* are totally subjective therefore. Those on earth are completely ignorant of the associations the departed may be making with them. And Buddhist teaching points out that it would not be good for the departed to really see and be in contact with the living. It would depress them, it is said, to see the continuing difficulties of those they loved.

There are different phases of *devachan* and the whole stay there may be very long. The idea, which one also finds in Steiner (see below, chapter 3) and in the New Testament ('There are many mansions in the House of my Father'), is that the departed rise gradually through *devachan*'s different levels until, eventually, the forces of *karma* come into play to determine the conditions of a new life, a new incarnation. The lapse of time between death and rebirth is very difficult to estimate, it is said, with any precision but traditionally it is thought to be rarely less than 1,500 years, except in special circumstances like cases of sudden death or death at a very young age. Some say that nowadays the period can be considerably shorter.

Why do Christianity and Islam (or Judaism) make no mention of reincarnation? Some maintain that in the time of Christ it was in fact a widely held belief. The disciples, when questioned by Jesus as to who he was, replied that some said he was John the Baptist, some said Elijah, some Jeremiah. And Christ's words about the man born blind suggest that they had a belief in reincarnation ('Master, who did sin, THIS MAN or his parents that he was born blind?'). It seems possible that reincarnation was proscribed by the first ecumenical council of the church at Constantinople in 553AD, though this is disputed.

It may also be that, like Buddhism in fact, both Christianity and Islam are essentially ethical religions that deal with how you behave and not philosophical constructs except in their more esoteric teachings perhaps. What is important in both these religions is the moral code you follow in your life not what you think in detail about the afterlife.

Whatever the 'soul' is, it is not what we know as the body and possibly not what we know as mind or intellect. The several religious texts referred to in this chapter would seem to indicate that in an afterlife there is a big question mark over the reality and objectivity of what we may see and do. The question of whether the 'soul' and personality are connected remains unclear, both in the western and the eastern religions. And yet it is surely a key issue. And linked to that is the question of the nature of consciousness after death. If we are to learn more about the meaning of death, and the inseparability of life and death, which we can observe constantly in the world around us, we need to be clearer about the nature of whatever it is that survives death. To that end we can try to find out something about the nature of the different states of the living and the dead for that should give a glimpse of the nature of what we could call 'soul-life'. And that is what the next chapter tries to do.

Chapter 3

The Living and the Dead

Different states

Rudolf Steiner was a Christian re-incarnationist. He was a scientist and philosopher and found over time that he had certain psychic abilities which allowed him the kind of visions and understanding that we might associate with the great mystics of the east. To many this is hard to swallow of course but maybe, the Hindu or Buddhist would tell us, all it takes is to imagine you developed a receptive power like the power of a transistor radio to capture sound or your satellite dish to capture TV signals. Not to mention the fact that everything that exists emits electromagnetic waves but only those that are hot (a light bulb, the sun) are visible to us. These waves surround us all and every day and all day, yet our own personal bodies cannot capture them (consciously). Maybe there are other waves in space that we can be trained to capture? Whatever the case, aside from his work in education which led to the Rudolf Steiner or Waldorf Schools, he lectured widely especially in Germany and Austria, and the topic of a number of his lectures was death and life, and the period between them.

While resolutely Christian, even if unconventional, Rudolf Steiner displays a fusion with what we usually see as more Oriental teachings. Much of what he has to say about periods after death is in harmony with esoteric Buddhism and its teachings about *kama loca* and *devachan* but also with what you can find in the Cabbala, the Jewish esoteric, mystical tradition. Steiner explains that there is a gradual development after death away from the connections with the material world into connections with the spiritual world. There are different levels in *kama loca* and in *devachan* (just as Jesus Christ described them in talking of the 'many mansions in the House of my Father'). After death and after an initial period of unconsciousness, consciousness returns and in *kama loca* we become engrossed with reflections on our past life; we will reflect upon and relive our relationships in life. But while we can change relationships while we are alive we can do nothing in *kama loca* but observe – and many times suffer regrets, painful regrets, at not having changed things while on earth. Steiner stresses again and again the importance of remaining conscious during these processes, of going through the periods after death with lucidity. We are likely to object that it might be better to be unconscious as we would then be likely to suffer less if at all. But Steiner says that with a dimming of consciousness 'the most terrible conditions of fear are connected'. It is of great importance, he goes on, that during life we practise and learn to maintain our consciousness at the moment of death. During these periods after death we have the feeling that we are becoming bigger and bigger and growing to occupy all of space; this is similar to the experiences described in The Tibetan Book of the Dead where the departed soul, on the first day, has a feeling of being in all space and of being centre and periphery at the same time. In fact, according to Steiner, what is happening is that in the *kama loca* period our soul gradually expands in space to encompass everything in our earth and moon system. In the *devachan* period our consciousness expands still further into the spheres of Mercury, Venus and the Sun in that order; all the while cutting off our bonds with the physical earth. Space travel, in other words... But as usual words distort a reality. Words, in this case the names of the planets, get in the way of our understanding. We are being told here that what happens is that our consciousness expands and expands and in that way we acquire a growing awareness of 'interconnectivity', how everything is connected in the universe even though there may be great distances between things – how everything is ONE. An electron on our planet for example can be in contact with an electron at the edge of the galaxy. This 'interconnectivity' is discussed in more detail in chapter 5 (see page 50) and in chapter 13 (see pages 144-145). What is perhaps particularly interesting in this interpretation is its similarity to the Cabbala. The Cabbala is a system of describing the visible and invisible worlds and the relationships between them. It is presented in the form of ten *sephirot* (see Fig. 1). Working from the bottom you move from the

Ain
Ain Soph
Ain Soph Aur

1.
Kether
the supreme crown (God)

3. Binah, understanding (Saturn) **2. Hokmah, wisdom (Uranus)**

5. Geburah, strength, rigor (Mars) **4. Heshed, mercy (Jupiter)**

6. Tiphereth, harmony (the Sun)

8. Hod, splendour (Mercury) **7. Netzach, beauty (Venus)**

9.Yesod, foundation (the moon)

10. Malkhuth, kingdom (the earth)

Figure 1: The 10 Sephirot

Earth through the Moon, Mercury, Venus, the Sun, Mars, Jupiter, Saturn and Uranus right up to the most spiritual and immaterial level which is the godhead. The only truly physical level, in our sense of the word, is the sephira Earth or *Malkhuth*. In a parallel representation the Cabbala sees all life as extending over four worlds from the least material, the highest spiritually, down to the physical world that we know. They are described as:

Olam Atsiluth – the world of spirit (Kether, Hokmah and Binah)

Olam Briah – the world of creation, of intelligence (Geburah, Heshed, Tipheret)
Olam Yetsirah – the world of formation, of construction (Hod, Netzach, Yesod)
Olam Assiah – the world of matter (Malkhuth)

Our existences are a movement from the highest down to the lowest and then up again. Hence the well-known *seal of Solomon* in which one triangle represents the descent into matter and the other the ascent from matter to spirit (Fig. 2).

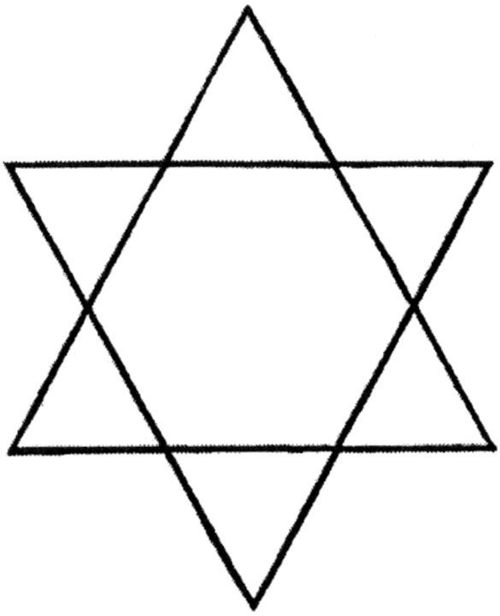

Figure 2: The Seal of Solomon

Rudolf Steiner speaks of the influence of the dead on the living and makes the point that particularly in the early period of *kama loca* the dead are likely to make more efforts to enter into contact with us, the living, than we are with them.

In some not very explicit pages in his collection of lectures 'Life between Death and Rebirth' he points out that there are times when the departed help us to avoid dangerous situations. He reminds us that for every event in our lives there are a lot of alternative events that COULD have happened. You drove yesterday to visit family in Leeds, some 100 miles of busy motorway in rainy weather. Everything went off well but at a certain point if you had been there a few minutes earlier there was a conjunction of circumstances that could have resulted in fatal accident. Steiner claims that a departed soul, dear to us, could have been the instrument that delayed our departure by a few minutes. In this way we never know, or are never fully aware of the vast number and nature of the alternatives that could have happened (see page 50 in chapter 5 about the plurality of worlds). 'Moments in which especially important things for us in the world of probability are taking place are also particularly favourable moments for the dead to draw near.'

Rudolf Steiner provides a lot of detail about the relationship between the living and the dead. I am reminded of some words of Sri Aurobindo, the founder of the ashram in Pondichery: 'At first sight it may appear that birth and death are attributes of life, but that isn't the case in reality for birth and death are processes belonging to matter, to the body.' Life does not stop, it continues, in other words. Steiner maintains that in the period, possibly several years, after death the dead remain close to those they were emotionally close to during their lives. The living can, by visualizing clearly the dead person, communicate with him or her. It is good, says Steiner, for people to be sociable in their lives because after death that makes for more closeness with the living and also for more contact with fellow souls in the other world; otherwise the soul can suffer great loneliness. After the moment of death and for a period of several of our earth days, the period that corresponds to the period of unconsciousness or coma in The Tibetan Book of the Dead, we are able to contemplate the tableau of our past life. It is important that the dead person should be able to fully concentrate on this tableau and not be distracted (by outpourings of grief among those left behind for example). On the lucid appreciation of one's past life future development will depend. As time passes, however, the departed soul moves further and further away from the earth and from its former personality and whatever contact with the living there may be becomes more tenuous and is eventually lost at least until the living themselves die.

Most of us, I think, have not experienced contact with the dead, and many would be sceptical. I personally had one experience only, but one which I find it difficult to reject. It was on the day of my father's death. I was working in a country some thousands of miles away and had gone for the weekend to a not very distant hotel intending to return to my apartment on the Sunday evening, in the meantime enjoying the usual luxuries of a four star hotel: cable TV, swimming pool, good food. On the Sunday morning I had been looking forward to spending most of the day there before going home and had arranged for a late check-out with Reception. But from mid-morning I unexpectedly found myself filled with a very powerful urge to go back to the apartment. At first I tried not to pay attention to it. But it was something very strong and irresistible; and seemed to be something that was growing from within me, taking me over, not allowing me to think about anything else, yet not coming from me. Before mid-day I gave in to it, checked out and went home. I had not been home for half an hour when my sister phoned to say our father had died that morning... What I experienced that day was so powerful that I still cannot help believing that my father was anxiously trying to contact me.

Many of the religions in our world have stressed and continue to stress the ethical aspect of our lives: how we should behave vis-à-vis our fellow-human beings. We find this in the Torah (where we find the Ten Commandments), in the Talmud, in Buddhism and the Noble Eightfold Path. Islam through the Koran gives a lot of guidance on how we should comport ourselves in family and society down even to detailed questions of inheritance, and has given rise to a whole system of law taught in universities in many Moslem countries – the *shari'a.* The

Buddha also, as already mentioned, as well as the Prophet Mohammed, made the point that it would take volumes of text and endless time to explain the metaphysics of our existence. This emphasis on behaviour is good, and necessary, even if at times it has been misused. Certainly behaviour is more important than knowledge. If we are to heed eastern teachings in particular and what people like Rudolf Steiner, working in a fusion of east and west, maintain, then the question of being able to pass through death is in the realm of behaviour: it has to do with our past behaviour and our future possible behaviour. It is not a question of knowledge. From this perspective what we do, our behaviour in life, is what constitutes the link between our life in our physical body and an afterlife. Knowledge alone cannot make that link. So it is important that we should not expect to live our life before and our life after death as two independent states: they are closely linked and interdependent. The question is, of course: what is meant by behaviour? That is not as simple as it may seem. 'Good' and 'bad' behaviours are not easily defined. What seems good could turn out to have perverse effects, and what seems bad may lead to something positive... Therefore this concentration on behaviour should be on acquiring an awareness of one's behaviour, observing it objectively and without judgement, doing everything with consciousness. Practising this during life is a form of preparation for what comes afterwards. It allows us to see more clearly and objectively what we were in our life.

Averroes, the 12th century Moslem philosopher, in his ponderings about the form we may take in resurrection concluded that it could not be in the physical form we now live in. This raises the whole question of the existence of forms other than what is physical and known to our physical sciences. And maybe a large part of what we call faith lies in the acceptance or refusal of this possibility. Yet, as pointed out above, we live surrounded by invisible waves of many kinds and can accept that without question. It is also worth remembering that even in science the invisible has a place. A virus has never been seen directly and can only be 'perceived' by means of an electron microscope. Anti-matter, by its very nature, is invisible. Many galaxies have not been seen by astronomers but are known to exist.

The Tibetan Book of the Dead, with the concept of the *bardo*, brings us face-to-face with the fact that the form of life after death is very different from what we know on earth and can be destabilizing. We see things very differently then. The Koran says: 'Indeed you were heedless of this. Now we have removed from you your covering, and sharp is your sight this Day!' (of Resurrection). 'You will no longer see through a glass darkly,' as the Bible says. But it is implied and in some cases explicitly stated that one needs some preparation for this. Otherwise, in the words of the Koran, 'the stupor of death will come in truth'. This is very explicit in The Tibetan Book of the Dead and as already mentioned Rudolf Steiner is also very clear that it is important to go through death with a lucid mind. The Upanishads – those very old Indian religious poems – likewise stress this. In *Isha*, at the end, the Upanishad repeats the ancient Hindu prayer of the dying: 'O Mind, remember Brahman, O Mind, remember thy past deeds.' The danger is, as emphasized by Steiner, that one could go through death in a kind of dream-like stupor and miss the opportunity to reflect clearly and vividly about how one has lived one's life. Above all missing the important connecting phase between life and death.

If all of this is so, then we have neglected in our modern way of life this matter of preparing for death. In our funeral ceremonies the focus is on what the participants say and do, though of course that may include prayers for the deceased. But sadly, perhaps, we have not made a place for any kind of prior preparation for death. Too often in our modern societies death comes suddenly, unexpectedly. Even when it does not, at the end of a long illness for example, the dying person is still kept in absolute unpreparedness for the event.

We can see a general consensus among varied beliefs that there is life after death. You don't have to a Christian, or a Moslem or a Jew or Buddhist to see that there is general agreement. Faith in a particular religion is not a prerequisite. Whether you are a Moslem or a Jew, a Christian or a Buddhist or a Hindu you have a life after death, that is what they all say. Although it has to be said that some restrict entry to their own community or at least to the community of 'believers' (cf. Islam). It is true that they don't all say exactly the same thing but the differences are in perspective.

We don't find a lot of clarity about what the 'soul' may be. But we do get the shared idea that life after death is VERY different and that while at first and even for several years there may be a possible closeness and even contact between the departed and the living, gradually these links fade and lose not only their physical but their emotional attachment. Just as they would for someone who has emigrated to a distant country. Over the years he or she grows away from their old country, they write less often, think about the old country less and less, memories fade, faces become more difficult to recall. For the departed, along with that gradual development away from the physical world, the earthly personality must also gradually lose its clarity and its reality. Very much in the same way that natural change is always gradual and slow.

None of this seems nonsensical. But if we are to probe more deeply into the question, which preoccupied Averroes, of the form we may have after death, we will have to face such concepts as permanence and impermanence. For if 'soul' there is, then it has to have some kind of permanence. This, however, is something that our minds have difficulty understanding, living as we do in a world where nothing is permanent.

Chapter 4

Things that Pass Away

Permanence and impermanence

The flat lands of south eastern Mali, near the borders with Ivory Coast and Burkina Faso, is a region of peasant farmers. Historically it has been a major cotton-producing area and while cotton is still grown there it is more and more difficult to compete in the world market. There have also been some recent gold finds but it is uncertain how much of the income earned from this mining finds its way back to the indigenous communities. In colonial days and in the years that immediately followed, the main cash crops were cotton and rubber which as well as enriching the trading houses of France allowed some profits to filter down to people in the region, making it one of the economically richest in the country. Apart from cotton and mining nowadays you will find mostly groundnuts, fruit such as mangoes, river fishing, cattle rearing and mainly subsistence farming. The Senoufo who live there, and in northern Ivory Coast and western Burkina Faso and who number around a million and a half, have the reputation of being hardy and courageous, strong-willed in the face of adversity. They were the last in Mali to hold out against the advance of French colonialism in the nineteenth century. The Senoufo have become well known for the quality of their art especially the carving of their wooden masks. These are always associated with the beliefs of the group which are passed on through the generations by a secret initiatic society called the *poro*. These beliefs are extremely sophisticated and merit study. The Senoufo believe that we possess an immaterial body, invisible usually to the naked eye, called the *nyil* which can travel outside you when you sleep. When you die you lose the *nyil* just as you do the physical body. But there is a part of you that cannot die, which they call the *pil*. The *pil* is part of *klé* or God. After death the *pil* goes to the village of the ancestors but we have to help it to get there by protecting it from the *nyil* now separated but still a threat.

Now the key points here are that there are three bodies, the physical body, the *nyil* and the *pil*. The *pil* is part of God, and that is important; they don't say it is the personality of the departed person or that it is a soul separate from God but that it is PART of God. (Note that in the Bhagavad-Gita – that very old, Hindu poem – we have Krishna saying: 'A spark of my eternal spirit becomes in this world a living soul.') Also the *pil* alone, not the *nyil*, goes to the village of the ancestors, the permanence of which is clearly implied. And the third point is that the *nyil* is somehow a threat after death. (The Bhagavad-Gita again: 'For thy soul can be thy friend and thy soul can be thine enemy.') We need to be protected from the *nyil* after death: it is something that can stop us from reaching the 'village of the ancestors'.

The Tibetan Book of the Dead, or *Bardo Thötröl* to give it its Tibetan name, is a guide to dying for us to be able to help a departed person in getting through the *bardo*, the phase after death when the departed finds him/herself in an unfamiliar, strange and somewhat frightening world (a more detailed account of this is to be found in chapter 2). The dying are constantly told in the *Bardo Thötröl* to avoid the soft lights of the jealous gods – the *nyils*? And the overall aim is to allow them to attain 'liberation' – like the village of the ancestors of the Senoufo? We find the same idea reflected in the Hindu masterpiece recounting the meeting of the Prince Arjuna with God, Krishna: 'The unwise think that I am that form of my lower nature which is seen by mortal eyes; they know not my higher nature, imperishable and supreme.'

Many belief systems or religions make a three-fold division of the human being (indeed of everything):

* Body
* Psyche, comprising feelings and intellect
* Spirit

And a distinction is made between the body and psyche which are said to belong to what is often termed the *personality*, which is transitory and impermanent and dies at death, whereas the spirit, in contrast, belongs to what we may call the *individuality*: it is what is permanent. In the beliefs of the Senoufo, the spirit is the *pil*, and it is part of God, part of the permanent. And the psyche, combining feelings and intellect, is the *nyil*. The psyche is not permanent and the *nyil* eventually disappears. But curiously it remains a danger for some time after death. Do we need to be told that our feelings and even our intellect present dangers? Our feelings and our intellect are not material so it is not unreasonable to suggest that they dissolve into nothingness more slowly that the material, physical body. The big issue is to know and to distinguish what is permanent and imperishable from what is doomed to pass away.

We all like to feel at peace with ourselves and with the world around us. While certainly there are times when we enjoy noise and being in a crowd we all without exception feel the need to be alone with ourselves and with nature, and feel that need to be something important. Whether we feel ourselves to be 'religious' or not, we are all sensitive to the feelings of peace, tranquillity and well-being that we experience on a mountain-top, by the sea listening to the sound of the waves, by a slow-flowing river, held in the spell of its unceasing movement and stillness, or contemplating the infinity and eternity of the night sky from a lonely country field.

At such times we experience a sort of escape into the present moment. Past and future cease to command our thoughts: so much of our time is spent obsessively reviewing the past and calculating the future! To be able to spend just some time contemplating something in the present without thinking of future results is a relief, a kind of bliss. The same can happen when we listen to music. We have the impression that we are finding another Ourself, not the one that is assailed by problems and demands, that is dissatisfied with what it does, is aggressive with colleagues, jealous, obsessed with success of different kinds, short-tempered, weakened by fears of many kinds.

We have to admit, however, that we generally do not dig very deeply into all these feelings. We suffer from a sort of 'laziness of the soul'. Something holds us back from looking more closely at our inner thoughts and feelings. The term was used by Steiner and this 'laziness of the soul' is part of our human condition. We have these feelings that seem transcendental from time to time but in the end we remain indifferent to their potential to affect us in any way that may change the way we see life. The truth is that, in our heart of hearts, we do not intend to spend a lot of time considering that kind of thing.

'When one sees eternity in things that pass away and infinity in finite things then one has pure knowledge.' We find those words in the Bhagavad-Gita, that dialogue already mentioned between the God Krishna and the prince Arjuna in which Krishna tries to get Arjuna to see what is true and real in our lives. But how can you find eternity in things that are impermanent and infinity in things that are finite? When I was a student, as I was leaving my room one afternoon in winter, to go to a lecture, a leafy branch on a stone wall in a lane I was walking along shook in the wind as I passed. It drew my attention; how or why I don't know but I was suddenly transfixed, for how long I don't know, experiencing infinity and eternity in those shaking leaves. An excursion into the present moment through a narrow opening that led to a different dimension of awareness. In a few leaves in the wind I saw all the continual movement, the constant becoming and unbecoming of everything that exists in the world we live in, and its eternal reality. Looking back on that experience what I remark now is that it began IN the world, in the world of impermanence, not in introspection or meditation or prayer. We have here a case of impermanence and eternity in one and the same object of perception. This paradox is of vital importance. But it is something that is impossible to express in words. There is something here of the paradoxes you find in Zen puzzles or *koans*. Zen Buddhism has its roots in this impossibility. Zen teachings and techniques abound in paradoxes and apparent nonsense. As Fritjof Capra pointed out regarding Zen: 'More than any other school of Eastern mysticism, Zen is convinced that words can never express the ultimate truth.' The underlying reality can only be reached through experience.

It is easy to describe what is impermanent in our lives, and it is possible to apprehend that in the impermanent, the movable, there is the buried, invisible presence of the permanent. It is quite another thing to describe the permanent. Perhaps it is best described by what it is NOT. We can try... It is not the physical body, of that we can be sure, the physical body like everything physical around us is doomed to disintegrate and disappear. Averroes, in 12th century Moslem Spain, spent much time meditating on whether we are to be resurrected in the physical body. With a feeling of some relief for he saw that could be a bore, he came to the conclusion that this was impossible and that resurrection must be in some other form. What about our feelings? Are they permanent? Hardly, judging by the way our moods and our affections and even our loyalties can swing. I think it was Jung who said: *You are not your emotions.* And indeed this point is used by councillors in helping people handle psychological trauma, such as sudden death by accident of a loved one. What about our thoughts? We tend to think our thoughts are a real part of us but are they? What is the reality? Is it not that when we are by ourselves we are constantly chattering to ourselves internally about this and that and all of those thoughts simply disappear and die, and from one hour to the other we would be incapable of recalling them? But we have more serious thoughts, of course. We have ideas and theories. But then scientists and researchers have observed that certain theoretical discoveries take place at the same historical time and in different places by people who have no contact with each other. The work on describing quanta done independently by Heisenberg and Schrödinger is sometimes quoted as an example, as is the simultaneous rediscovery of calculus in England and Germany and elsewhere. A less known example is that of the Russian engineer, Popov, who successfully carried out an experiment in wireless telegraphy in the Russia of Tsar Nicholas in 1894, almost a year before Marconi. As if ideas were around and about us and, at a certain time, became ripe for capture. So what we take for OUR ideas may not be ours at all.

There is a Buddhist meditation which goes like this:

> The physical body: this is not mine, this am I not, this is not my soul.
> My feelings: These are not mine, these am I not, these are not my soul.
> My thoughts: These are not mine, these am I not, these are not my soul.
> My mental states: These are not mine, these am I not, these are not my soul.
> My ego: This is not mine, this am I not, this is not my soul.

Fifteen or twenty minutes' inward repetition of this formula leads us on a path away from the changeable and the impermanent. For it focuses our mind on the fact that the body will eventually die and decompose, that our feelings come and go, our thoughts likewise (and with great rapidity), and our mental states such as animosity, well-being, depression, jealousy are also subject to change. That even our ego, our personality, cannot be permanent in any sense.

The Cabbala, the esoteric philosophy behind Judaism, has a neat way of representing impermanence and permanence. And it represents the difference not by showing them as black and white, binary opposites, but more of a sliding scale. If you look at the diagram (see chapter 3, page 31) of the ten *sephirot* (plural of sephira) you will see that they stretch from the lower one, Malkhuth, which is our physical world, through Yesod, which is our emotions, Hod which is our thinking processes and further and further up through Heshed which is our ideas of justice and universal love, to the creative principle, God to Christians, Brahman to Hindus, *Yahweh* to Jews, and *Allah* to Muslims. So, just to take the *sephirot* mentioned, what is in Malkhuth, the physical world is obviously impermanent, what is in the emotional world, Yesod, is also impermanent but less material. Our thoughts in the world of Hod are more long-lasting but also impermanent in time, our ideas of justice, universal love in the sephira Heshed are more permanent still, but it is only when you get to Kether, the creator, the Emanator, that we reach any idea of a kind of genuine permanence, of eternity. But, and this is interesting, it doesn't stop there. Beyond the highest *sephira*, Kether, there are other levels which are:

Ain Soph Aur: Light without End
Ain Soph: Without End
Ain: Without

So there's the answer. Real permanence is nothingness! Nothing we can see, hear, touch, smell or taste. And indeed that's all it can be. If it were something it wouldn't be permanence!

Obviously we are up against the question of what is meant by 'something'. To return to paradoxes there is a sense in which something can be nothing and nothing something. If you meditate on the Buddhist prayer on page 43 and slowly divest yourself, so to speak, of your physical body, its pleasures, illnesses and frailties, of your feelings, of hates and loves, of obsessions, of enthusiasms, of shame, of fears and hopes, of wishes and urges, of your complexes, your ego and your self-importance, your disappointments and resentments, passions and affections, grudges, jealousies, thoughts, ideas, theories, ideologies and causes, your education and erudition, you are still left with something. Something very difficult to define but which is the something that underlies all existence. I think that is a first step to understanding permanence.

Chapter 5

The Veil of Illusion

Things are not at all what they seem

We sit here in our chair, reading a book, secure in our world of solid and well-known objects, secure in the knowledge that we can deal with any unknown objects we come across and bring them within our comprehension. But if we look at what the physicists and mathematicians following on Einstein and Heisenberg, Schrödinger, Dirac and others have to tell us about the structure of the atomic and sub-atomic universe our certainties are likely to be shaken.[1] The 18th century Scottish philosopher, David Hume, minimalist and sceptic, is reported to have said, possibly on a good day: 'Mankind are nothing but a bundle or collection of different perceptions in perpetual flux and movement.' True enough, but if Hume had been abreast of the findings of physics and mathematics in the twentieth century he would have seen that it is much more complex than he imagined. He would in fact have found himself face-to-face with a few unexpected philosophical problems.

Modern physics has uncovered some very strange behaviour at the level of particles. For one thing light, which had been thought to be composed of particles, turned out to be both particles and waves. The distinction between particles and waves had until then seemed radical, there could be no confusing them. But actually determining when we are dealing with particles and when we are dealing with waves has turned out to be not easy. And yet a wave stretches on forever whereas a particle is limited and well-defined in space. The definite and the infinite, no two things could be more dissimilar.

'Where one sees nothing but the One, hears nothing but the

One, knows nothing but the One – there is the Infinite. Where one sees another, hears another, knows another – there is the finite. The Infinite is immortal, the finite is mortal.' (Upanishads, *Chandogya*) But what if one can become the other?

So particles and waves can be confused. But which is more real, the particle or the wave? You will get different answers depending on how you look at them. When, in an experiment, light is passed through two slits onto a screen and the *result* of the trajectory of the electrons is registered we find, to our amazement, on studying the evidence of how the light hits the screen, that the same particle seems to go through two holes at the same time! In other words the electron behaves like a wave, but when we try to observe an electron in movement it behaves like a particle. When we look closely at which hole it goes through it goes through only one hole and ignores the other but when we don't look at its passage it seems to know that there are two holes and goes through both at the same time. We can only know where things are when we are looking at them. A moment's inattention and they disappear. Thus the observer is an integral part of the event he/she observes. And the puzzles don't stop there. Experiments have shown that every time the universe is faced with a choice at the quantum level it divides itself into two universes and both options are selected. This leads to the existence of many alternatives to every action, each having a real existence. In the experiment where light was sent through two slits we have to observe the electron all the time to know which hole it went through. But then if we don't observe it, it goes through both so it makes no sense to say it went through one or the other. In John Gribbin's words, 'Its trajectory has got to be the sum of both trajectories.'

In the old days it was thought that there were only four particles in the universe: the electron, the proton, the neutron and the photon. The core of the atom consisted of positively charged protons and electrically neutral neutrons. Electrons, negatively charged, gravitated around the core. The photon is an elementary particle that transports electromagnetic radiation. Developed by Einstein the concept of the photon helped account for the fact that light COULD be particles and not waves as previously thought. There were also two basic forces: gravity and electromagnetism. It is now clear that there are many kinds of particles and that two extra forces exist called the weak force and the strong force. The strong force is what allows particles to hold together. The electromagnetic force can explain how two electrons with negative charges can interact with protons in a nucleus that is positively charged and maintain stability (not tear apart). But it cannot explain how several protons (which are positively charged) can exist together in a nucleus without being forced apart. The strong force holds them together.

'Beta decay' is an event where a neutron isolated from the nucleus will decay into an electron and a proton within a few minutes, but the resulting mass is much less than the original neutron. Where did the extra mass go? This 'decay', it was realized, pointed not only to the existence of another particle but to that of another force. And this other particle must have zero mass or it would have been observed. A new theory was required to explain this phenomenon for it was not due to electromagnetism or gravity; nor was it the strong nuclear force for it was known that electrons didn't react to the strong force. And so the 'weak force' was discovered and the mysterious particle was called a *neutrino*, in fact an 'anti-particle'. The weak field is very important in nuclear fusion, in the energy created by the sun and the devastating power of nuclear weapons.

Particles can be classified into those that 'feel' the strong force, called fermions and those that don't, called bosons. Fermions cannot be created or destroyed whereas bosons *can* be created and destroyed. In this way there are, on the one hand, particles that produce the material world and, on the other hand, particles that hold it together by producing the interactions that create stability (or in certain cases break it apart). So one can say that matter and force are two faces of the same thing even if this is counter-intuitive. Every fermion in the universe has a bosonic partner and every boson has a fermion as partner, and these partners are invisible to us. Thus what we see around us in our everyday lives is only HALF the universe. And one result of what became the string theory is that there would be two universes interpenetrating other. In the words of John Gribbin:

> The result would be two universes, interpenetrating one another but interacting only through gravity – our world and a so-called 'shadow universe'. There would be shadow photons, shadow atoms, perhaps even shadow stars and shadow planets, inhabited by shadow people existing in the same space-time that we inhabit, but invisible. A shadow planet could pass right through the Earth and never affect us, except through its gravitational pull. It sounds like science fiction, but one reason that the idea has been taken seriously is that there is astronomical and cosmological evidence that a lot of the universe exists in the form of dark matter, detected gravitationally but not seen.

It was the British physicist, Paul Dirac, who first put forward the hypothesis, since then accepted as real, that all particles of the material world have their counterparts in the form of anti-matter, mirror-image particles. When a particle meets its anti-matter partner it disintegrates.

This distinction between fermions which cannot be created or destroyed, and bosons, which can, is fundamental in modern physics. Yet physicists will now say they are interchangeable, that one can become the other. In the same way that particles can be waves and waves particles.

All of that is part of the effort to find a mathematical description which will account for everything. More recent attempts to elaborate this Grand Unified Theory uniting in one equation the behaviour of all particles and of the four known forces have led to the proposal that there are up to eleven dimensions needed to explain the universe! We are conscious of only four! And where on earth are those other dimensions?

Physicists explain that they must have folded in upon themselves to become invisible in our four-dimensional world. It is a case of compactification hiding the other dimensions.

> The analogy is often made with a hosepipe. From a distance a hosepipe looks like a wiggly line, a one-dimensional object. But closer up you can see that it is a two-dimensional object. Every point on the wiggly line is actually a circle, a loop around the point, and the cylinder is the string of all these circles, one behind the other.
> (John Gribbin, In Search of SUSY, page 110)

But when we talk of fermions and bosons, of electrons, neutrons and protons, as if they were distinct lumps of matter we must remember quantum mechanics and that we only see what we observe, that a thing can be two things at the same time, and that when we don't see it, it both exists and doesn't exist (at the same time). And, to add to that, when we do look at it we change it!

It requires a few minutes of quiet thought to allow the idea to sink in that all this activity of particles interacting, destroying each another, creating new particles, and of interacting forces, is taking place at every moment in our own bodies and in the world we can see around us. And one might care to bear in mind also that there are conditions in which an electron can interact with another electron ANYWHERE in the universe…

This foray into quantum mechanics could lead any normal thinking person to give up looking for any spirituality in life. Yet some scientists, for example Fritjof Capra (in his book *The Tao of Physics)*, have tried to show that the two can join. The difficulty is twofold. It is with the words we use and with the concepts we try to share. One of the reasons, I suggest, why many people reject the idea of, say, a world of spirits, of the existence of angels, of a god, is not just materialism but the fact that we tend to personify these concepts and those personifications grow out of the simple images of our childhood. We tend to try to think of them in terms of persons and bodies which leads to all sorts of illusions. We need perhaps to be prepared to see 'reality' totally differently. Whatever may exist beyond what we can see with our human eyes and hear with our human ears does not have the kind of physical reality that for us, in what has got to be our illusion, corresponds to the usual objects of those organs. And the words that we may use (angels, spirits, God, among others) are words used to describe things outside our observable world and even outside our dimensions.

The *Book of Tao* by Lao Zi was written in China in the sixth century before our era and is the basis of the Tao philosophy. There are many lines from the Tao which sum up the elusiveness of the invisible reality that lies below everything in existence. Here are a few:

> All is peace, quietness and security.
> Sound of music, smell of good dishes
> Will make the passing stranger pause.
> How different the words the Tao gives forth!
> So thin, so flavourless!
> If one looks for Tao there is nothing solid to see;
> If one listens for it there is nothing loud enough to hear.
> If one uses it, it is inexhaustible.

And is that not similar to what physicists are looking for in their search for the 'theory of everything', a superforce which would underlie the four basic forces, gravity, electromagnetism, strong and weak nuclear forces? The theory that would eliminate all contradictions between relativity and quantum mechanics, that would unite the infinitely large and the infinitely small.

One thing, however, is more than certain. What we take for reality is less real than we imagine. The world we live in has a reality different from what we see or think we see. Things are definitely not what they seem.

Chapter 6

Reaching for the Self

Behind the veil

How many of us become truly aware of our own unreality? Some only, I think. For most of us, and for all of us in at least a part of our lives, we spend our time creating an artificial reality, perceived by an artificial personality which (we are dimly aware) is of no permanence. But that doesn't matter; as long as today is real, or seems so, who cares about tomorrow?

Different religions use different words to describe the underlying reality. *Tao* is the same as the Dharmakaya of the Vedas of ancient India, the clear light of the Void (Mahayana Buddhism), it is the *sat*, the Absolute or Spirit Divine of Hinduism, Allah Lord of the Worlds (Koran 1.2), the Word of Christianity, the ultimate reality underlying everything. In these matters we are up against the limitations of language. Language is inadequate to describe things that are, well, multi-dimensional. And thus the attempts to render the incomprehensible by breaking the conventions of language as a conveyor of logic. Language is linear, reality is not. Zen has always tried to go beyond linear meaning. Huxley quotes a Zen Master:

> Having swept everything clean before you, Secho now opens a passage-way, saying: 'Do you understand or not? An iron bar without a hole.' He has done all he could for you; he is exhausted – only able to turn round and present you with this iron bar without a hole. It is a most significant expression. Look and see with your own eyes! If you hesitate you miss the mark forever.

There is obviously something not logical about this. Zen, as Huxley observes, tries to stimulate the mind to go beyond sense. Logic, in other words, cannot provide the answers. The question then is: what can? What can help us to understand our relationship to the underlying reality?

Issues of immanence and transcendence are ways of characterizing beliefs. Christianity, Judaism and Islam are transcendent religions – excluding some of their more mystical derivations. God is conceived as being above us, outside us, and makes himself manifest to us through prophets or visions. Eastern religions are both transcendent and immanent for God is seen as existing also inside us. It is the *Atman* and *Brahman* of Hinduism where *Brahman* is the God outside us, the ultimate, and *Atman* is the reflection of that God within us.

Of course the word 'God' itself produces many problems of communication and meaning. Some see God as a person who watches you, keeps you, protects you, listens to you, talks to you. Once in China I was travelling on a coach beside a Westerner of around 55, who was, I think, a very religious person and maybe a clandestine missionary of some sort. We talked amiably for some hours on that long journey and towards the end of it I asked him what had brought him to China. 'God told me to come,' was his reply. Now, I don't think (though I can't be sure) that he was telling me that God actually spoke to him with a human voice and gave him that advice. I think rather that he had what he felt to be an inner voice which directed him towards that decision. But for him that inner voice came from God. Averroes, or Ibn Rushd, that twelfth century Moslem philosopher from Cordoba, has some thoughts on God speaking to us. He does not refute the idea that it is possible. God must in one way or another have a power equivalent to speech or he would be unable to perform something that mortals can perform. But, talking of God communicating to us, Averroes goes on to say that this kind of communication might come from the 'intermediary of an angel' or 'by revelation', or it might be through an utterance which the receiver hears as if by chance. God does not speak directly to mortals, says Averroes quoting the Koran, except 'by revelation or behind a veil', or by sending a messenger in some form or another. Of revelation he writes: 'Revelation, then, is the creation of that meaning in the soul of the person receiving it without the intermediary of utterances created by Him.'

The prophets Moses and Abraham received their revelations from an Angel or Archangel, as did Mohammed. As did Mary. Adam, in the Cabbalistic tradition, received the book containing the secrets of creation, the *Sephir Yetsirah* (later taken away from him) from the Archangel *Raziel.* Saint Teresa of Avila, in her autobiography, comments on the fact that she found herself reading the Confessions of Saint Augustine as if by chance: 'It seems to me that the Lord commanded it for I didn't find them myself nor had I ever seen them.'

My fellow traveller in China had the conviction that the idea which prompted him to come to China had been planted in his mind by God. One can pooh-pooh this as being the result of some movements in the unconscious mind that lead to a particular choice. But it does raise questions. For instance what if we were to ask if the same was not true of Moses and other prophets? Perhaps they too were kidding themselves thinking that God was speaking to them, even if through an angel. The problem is (is it not?) that in all these cases we are thinking of some personal God figure outside ourselves and existing in time. It might pay to look at these experiences from another angle.

A distinction has been drawn between our personality and our individuality. The personality is the persona that we have created for ourselves, how we see ourselves, how we want others to see us, how others see us. It is unstable, likely to change, rooted in our needs and desires, fears and other emotions, and generally the source of a lot of unhappiness for us. The individuality, on the other hand, is the part of us that corresponds to our ideals, our altruism, our sense of sacrifice, our compassion for mankind and its suffering. Above all it is that part that is not diminished by concerns like praise or blame, comfort or discomfort, making money or losing money, pleasantness or unpleasantness; it is beyond these concerns. When touched by our individuality we have a sense of permanence and of being beyond time. It is useful to compare this to the Self of the Hindu writings. 'He who dwells in the mind but is separate from the mind, whom the mind does not know, whose body the mind is, and who controls the mind from within – he, the Self, is the Inner Ruler, the Immortal.'

So another way of putting it would be to say that it is the Self that speaks to us from within our mind and gives us paths to follow. Let's not forget that in Hinduism the Atman, or Self, and Brahman, God, are one. The Sufi al-Halladj said: 'I have become one with the One I love (God)'; in other words his personality has yielded its place to his individuality or his Self. This did not go down well with his contemporaries and he was executed for heresy.

There are different ways of describing this Self of course, words are only words. In the Koran: 'Is he who was dead and We gave him life and set for him a light whereby he can walk amongst men, like him who is in the darkness from which he can never come out? Thus it is made fair-seeming to the disbelievers that which they used to do.'

The man who is 'dead' is he whose mind is in darkness and who lives only in the personality; the *light* that God gives is the awakened soul or the Self which guides men through the mists of life. The unbelievers who don't believe in the Self, in the God-impulse, live in the personality which is always tempting us with bright knick-knacks and passing pleasures (is 'fair-seeming').

There is an interpretation of the Nativity which sees it as a symbolic representation of the birth of the Inner Self. In this interpretation the historical decor of the stable, manger, donkey and cow are to be seen symbolically. The birth of the child Jesus is the birth of the Inner Self which can come to all of us. The stable, the humble place where the child Christ is brought into the world, is the lower abdomen of us humans, what in the Orient they call the *hara centre,* the seat of the Self. In this way the birth of Jesus is a symbolic representation of the realization of the Self.

In the Upanishads, in *Chandogya,* the Self is described from another perspective. When the Self is associated with the senses, it says, we experience pleasure and pain, but once we get beyond the senses we no longer experience pleasure or pain in the same way. 'Rising above consciousness, knowing the Self to be distinct from the senses and the mind, knowing it in its true light, one rejoices and is free.'

There is a vivid and moving depiction of this contrast between the personality and the individuality in the description of Jesus' inner struggle in the garden of Gethsemane. Contemplating the suffering he will have to endure in the coming hours and filled with a chilling fear and a wish to live not die, Jesus has a moment of weakness in which the personality comes to the fore. For a moment he refuses his role. 'O Father, if it be possible, let this cup pass from me.' But the Self reasserts itself: 'Nevertheless not as I will but as Thou wilt.' The individuality, the Inner Self, is one with the will of God. A reassuring piece of evidence, nevertheless, that even great sages have their human weaknesses.

If we follow this line of thinking, the voice that spoke to my companion on that bus journey was the voice of the individuality, the underlying permanent reality within him as within all of us. Of course that inner voice doesn't speak to us regularly and doesn't speak to all of us. It can however come into our lives unexpectedly and in special circumstances.

The day was hot but not hot enough to make the beach near Dakar unpleasant. We had the beach to ourselves, apart from a small group of people visible in the distance to the east there was nobody. The sea was calm and we had all spent at least an hour in it. We found a place sheltered from the fairly mild wind, just behind a dune for a picnic lunch of salad and sandwiches with a glass of wine. After the lunch it was still not too hot to keep the children from deciding to go again for a swim. Off they went with our encouragement. We were in the shelter of the dune and they were not immediately visible to us as they jumped around in the waves at the edge of the sea. We could hear their laughter as a background to our own conversation with our friends.

Just as when you wake up you become only slowly conscious that the noise you hear is the alarm clock, so it was not immediately that we noticed a change in the sounds reaching us from the beach. The cries coming from the children had changed in tone – dramatically. There was a shrillness in them, pain and panic. Everything happened so quickly then. Bits of what happened are wiped from my memory. The next thing I remember is coming close to the children, running fast, and my elder daughter was running towards us herself shouting with tears in her voice, 'Helena (the other daughter) is drowning!' We could see quickly that Helena was out in the waves and that my 13 year old son had jumped in to try to reach her and was himself struggling. All of these things registered at once and simultaneously. Clearly there had been a sudden change in the sea for a dangerous set of huge waves was now pounding the beach and the noise of the sea drowned out all else; the drama at this spot on the beach and the shouts could not have been audible to the small group not so far away to the east. It was not immediately that I realized that I had not stopped running but had plunged into the waves and ploughed towards the children.

I found myself unable to do anything useful and was myself swiftly swept out until my wife and friends left on the beach had become distant figures. I was to learn later that my younger daughter had been carried back to land by a large wave and that my son had got back as well by, as he explained proudly, 'swimming underwater'.

I spent a long time in the sea making many attempts to get back to land where one of my friends had managed to get a few yards into the waves on a spit of sand and was holding out a hand to me. Several times I came within inches of that hand only to be swept far out again. Obviously I was becoming exhausted and after one more futile attempt to get back I found myself again out at sea. I became aware of the hopelessness of my situation, and even had a moment's panic when I thought about sharks. But then, suddenly and to my amazement, now, I found myself able to contemplate the situation with what I can only describe as serenity. It occurred to that it was ironic that I should die in the sea as my father had done. I knew that my family would be deeply affected but also knew they would get over it. It was as if a second me had taken over, a bigger me, a better me. I was outside the smaller things of life, I was in a different dimension with different values. Life seemed something fairly trivial. There was no fear, only a sort of tranquil, all-knowing acceptance. I think that day I had an encounter with the fringes of the Self.[1]

They say that if you want to feel the presence of the Self you should meditate and concentrate your mind on your occiput for five or ten minutes, without any other thoughts interfering. But, as is always the case with these exercises, they warn that you should not do it for too long or too often. There is a degree of danger involved, but less perhaps than in an untamed sea off Senegal.

Still the experiences of underlying permanence and of the 'individuality' in this chapter remain fragmentary and involuntary, even if intuitively attractive. The case needs to be more solid to be truly acceptable. And that problem is what the second part of this book will address.

Part Two

Desperately Seeking Permanence

Chapter 7

A Man Called Gilgamesh

One man's quest for immortality

For most of us, when we are born into this world, the first thing we perceive is a blast of brilliant light, which must be extremely painful to our new eyes. If we are to accept Tolstoy's telling of Anna Karenina's death another blast of dazzling light will blind us at the moment of our death and our passage into what lies beyond it. It has got to be true that since time immemorial we human beings, observing the reality of death around us, must have constantly asked ourselves what, if anything, is permanent in the human being. The mystery of death has been a preoccupation of every civilization and culture on the face of this earth.

Our obsession with death is tied up with two other issues. One is the existence or not, and if it exists, the nature, of the human soul. The other issue is ethical: how should one live one's life? What is the role of man in society? What are his duties and responsibilities? And what would be the effects of this role on life after death? Society needs rules; religions came up with rules. Some rules are shared by all religions, some are particular to one religion. It does not make life easier.

The content of the previous chapters had mainly to do with death, and with permanence and impermanence. But it is important to look again and more closely at the ideas that mankind has come up with as regards the nature of what we may call the soul, for understanding the possible nature of a 'soul' seems essential to trying to comprehend permanence. And if we look at what different traditions have to say about the 'soul' we may find that they are more similar than we might have thought.

Before that, however, it is worth looking at an account of one man's quest for immortality, buried in an ancient myth. It was over two thousand years before our era, in Sumeria, modern-day Iraq, in a period of time situated between Abraham and Noah, that a masterpiece of Babylonian literature, the Epic of Gilgamesh, was composed. When I looked again at this piece of world literature I discovered to my surprise that there were other messages in it, messages that were very relevant to the topic of death. It is a story in which death and the afterlife are central. Gilgamesh, a prince, 'two thirds god and one third man', is obsessed by two things: his mortality, and the need to leave something permanent and grand so that his name would live forever. 'Only the gods live forever but as for us men, our days are numbered and our occupations are a breath of wind.' The story tells us of Gilgamesh's relationship with Enkidu who was originally sent by the gods to fight him and destroy his pride. However, Enkidu becomes a dear friend. Then Enkidu dies and Gilgamesh's love for him is so strong and this loss so painful that 'he began to rage like a lion, like a lioness robbed of her whelps'. Enkidu's death brings home to Gilgamesh, with brutality, the horror of separation from one's loved ones and the fact that he must sooner or later follow the same route. He decides to go and find the mysterious Utnapishtim, called 'the Faraway', who is known to be the only man to enter the realm of the gods and so become immortal. And this is where the epic of Gilgamesh reaches its most interesting point – and its most mysterious. Every detail is now important and potentially full of meaning.

In order to get to the place where Utnapishtim dwells Gilgamesh has to overcome many trials, including a long period in a wilderness and a fight with three lions. He eventually comes to Mount Mashu where the sun sets. Here he meets the horrific 'scorpion-men' who, though terrifying, recognize the god-element in Gilgamesh and give him directions. He travels for twelve 'double-hours' through impenetrable darkness before coming into a beautiful garden filled with light with the 'tree of the gods bearing fruit on its branches of lapis-lazuli'. Here there is what can only be a goddess, in the person of Siduri, a maker of wine, who hides herself, frightened by Gilgamesh's wild appearance. Eventually she listens to him but tells him: 'Gilgamesh, where are you hurrying to? You will never find that life for which you are looking. When the gods created man they allotted him death, but life they retained in their own keeping.' She advises him to enjoy life, eat, dance and be merry. But such advice is meaningless to Gilgamesh. He tells her he knows that to get to Utnapishtim he has to cross an ocean. The goddess tells him that it is a very perilous crossing. But she says he can go and see the ferryman of Utnapishtim and perhaps that man will agree to ferry him across the ocean. She reminds him that 'with him (the ferryman) are the holy things, the things of stone', and that the ferryman was fashioning 'the serpent prow of the boat'. 'Look at him well,' advises the goddess. Gilgamesh goes there, smashes the holy things of stone by the river, finds the ferryman and 'looks him in the eye'. The ferryman listens to his story but tells him that as he has smashed the holy things of stone he has destroyed the safety of the boat. Gilgamesh is given a seemingly impossible task by the ferryman. 'Go into the forest and with your axe cut poles, one hundred and twenty, cut them sixty cubits long, paint them with bitumen, set them on ferrules and bring them back.' Gilgamesh does as told. They then launch out on the waters of the ocean until they reach the 'waters of death'. From then on Gilgamesh has to use the one hundred and twenty poles he has cut to propel the boat but using each pole only once and not allowing his hands to touch the water. When he has used the last pole, number one hundred and twenty, he strips himself, holds up his 'arms for a mast and his covering for a sail.' And so he was brought to where Utnapishtim dwelled.

There are so many things in this tale that are obviously symbols and which concentrate our attention, pushing us to attempt some interpretation. What Gilgamesh undertook was demanding, it required all his attention and strength, and in this way it is reminiscent of the trials that a would-be initiate had to go through in ancient Egypt or ancient Greece. He had first to survive the long period of wandering in the wilderness after Enkidu's death which marked the end of his perfect friendship. Then the three lions he comes across on a mountaintop and which he kills. In the text the lions seem to have a link to the Moon. We can say that the Moon represents what is transitory, what is illusion or dream and so represents the illusion of the unreality that we live in. Slaughtering the lions, which are 'glorifying in life' according to the text, is accepting that life is a dream. After this episode, and only then, he arrives at the twin peaks of Mount Mashu and at its gates are the scorpion-men. In astrology the scorpion is always associated with death, with the eighth house, the house of death. The scorpion-men are terrifying in appearance but like the terrifying visions in the Tibetan Book of the Dead they turn out to be harmless. With their natural clairvoyance (the scorpion being associated with death is at one and the same time in the world of the living and the world of the dead) they see the god-element in him and give him directions. But they first warn him that it is a futile journey and that it means going through a place of no light where 'the heart is oppressed with darkness', and where no mortal man has ever gone. Their attempts to discourage Gilgamesh fail and they give him permission to 'pass through the mountain'. Then follows the impenetrable darkness he has to go through, seemingly without hope of emerging from it. But at last, after 'seeing nothing ahead and nothing behind him' for mile after mile, he emerges into the sunlight and a garden of the gods. The tree in the garden of the gods has fruit of carnelian and leaves of lapis lazuli. Like all gems lapis lazuli must have some significance, which we cannot fully know now, except to remark that it was, like carnelian, much used by Egyptians. Gilgamesh comes across Siduri the wine-maker, but why wine? Just because it symbolizes the pleasures of life? Or something more? Wine is, as Christianity tells us, associated with life itself, with the secret of life; the seed contained in the grape is a perfect symbol of the male sexual organ. And what of the stones that Gilgamesh smashes, the 'holy things'? Gilgamesh smashes the stones 'in anger'. It is not clear why. Either there is something missing here or the explanation was clear to a reader of the time. Was he angry because Siduri had told him that if it proved not possible to cross the waters he would have to return to wherever he came from? He saw the stones perhaps as representing old beliefs that needed to be replaced, got rid of. Or perhaps the act of smashing the stones reveals Gilgamesh's human weakness in giving way to unreasonable anger and foretells that he can never gain immortality. We could also think that if Gilgamesh was angry at that moment perhaps the stones told the tale of things that drove him to distraction like the futility and brevity of human life. From what the ferryman told him we understand that there is a connection between the stones and the boat, by smashing the stones he had destroyed the safety of the boat. And stones of course are the most permanent manifestation of matter. Then there is the mystery of the number of poles he has to cut: one hundred and twenty each 'sixty cubits long.' Why are the figures so precise?

The ferryman is fashioning 'the serpent prow of a boat'. Snakes are always symbolic of the visible and invisible worlds, and of the gift of prophecy. The text is very clear that Gilgamesh must look straight at the ferryman 'in the eye'. This is obviously important in some way but the sense is now unclear to us. It looks as if it symbolizes some contract passed with the ferryman.

This density of symbolism is very tantalizing though extremely difficult to interpret but things become even more mysterious when Utnapishtim reveals the secret given to him and how he deserved it. It may be that a close examination of this part gives us the keys also to the details of the journey of Gilgamesh to the place where Utnapishtim lived.

The ferry brought Gilgamesh to the place where Utnapishtim, the only mortal 'to whom the gods had given everlasting life', was reclining at his ease, but, intrigued by the arrival of this stranger, he asked abruptly what had brought him there. Gilgamesh tells his story and explains that he is afraid himself of death. Utnapishtim assures him that 'there is no permanence'. Gilgamesh asks him outright to tell him how he came 'to enter the company of the gods and to possess everlasting life'. And Utnapishtim, aware now of all the trials that Gilgamesh has gone through, reveals to him 'a mystery, a secret of the gods'.

Utnapishtim then relates a story of a flood, not at all dissimilar in its narrative to the story of Noah. The gods had decided to let loose a deluge on the city of Shurrapak, but the god Ea, a god of wisdom associated with water, warned Utnapishtim in a dream. The god told him to tear down his house and build a boat. And gave very precise instructions about the measurements of the boat. There is a very detailed description for the building of the boat into which Utnapishtim put his family, all the craftsmen and 'the beasts of the field wild and tame'. The storm and rain lasted six days and at the end of it no living creature was left on earth. Several days later, after releasing a dove, which returned, then a swallow, which returned, Untapishtim released a raven, which didn't return. They had survived! Utnapishtim offered the usual sacrifices. The gods were attracted by the smell of the libations. They quarrelled among themselves. Ishtar blamed Enlil for needlessly causing the flood – the faults of humanity could have been corrected less violently. Enlil is furious at finding Utnapishtim has survived but when Ea explains that he did not reveal the secret of the gods, but 'the wise man learned it in a dream', Enlil forgets his anger and grants everlasting life to Utnapishtim.

But what exactly was 'the secret of the gods' that is mentioned several times? Can it be that it is hidden in the story of the building of the boat?

Ea gave very detailed instructions about the boat. Those instructions were followed to the letter. Utnapishtim did exactly as he was told.

In some of the more esoteric interpretations of the book of Revelation the New Jerusalem is not a place but is a symbol of the temple we are to make of our bodies. But this is not a physical body as Saint Paul, a Jew presumably familiar with the Greek and Egyptian Mysteries as well as the Cabbala, makes clear in one of his letters, 'there are heavenly bodies and there are earthly bodies'. What dies is physical, and 'weak and ugly', what is everlasting is 'beautiful and strong'. 'There is of course,' he writes, 'a physical body, so there has to be as spiritual body.'

Saint Paul tries to explain that what we do in this life, our actions, are impermanent and bound to death and from this death, as from a seed, the new body, the spiritual body comes into being.

'So also is the resurrection of the dead. It is sown in corruption; it is raised in incorruption. (…) It is sown in a natural body, it is raised in a spiritual body'. Averroes, writing in Cordoba, in 12th century Moslem Spain, points out that of course all religions agree on the idea of resurrection but the problem is that there are different perceptions as to the *mode.* Arguing in logical, Aristotelian terms he concludes that it cannot be in a physical body – which is by nature subject to dissolution – and so there must be a spiritual body. And so, he goes on, 'There are two kinds of happiness accessible to mankind, one is otherworldly and the other is this worldly.' This would seem to imply two different ways of perceiving. We find this also in Saint Paul: 'For now we see things as through a glass, darkly; but then face to face; now I know in part; but then I shall know even as also I am known.' This possibility that there must be different ways of perceiving this life and another life seemed to be important. And not surprising for the instruments of perception in our physical life, our eyes, our intellect, may not be appropriate outside it.

Other faculties, appropriate to a non-physical body, need to be deployed.

It is interesting that Freemasons use the same symbolism as Gilgamesh; for them man has to be the builder of his own spiritual temple using certain tools and certain methods. Let's not forget that origins of the teachings of freemasonry are possibly as old as the Epic of Gilgamesh.

And so what if the boat of Utnapishtim represents a spiritual body, which has to be constructed following certain exact instructions? He is told to destroy his old house, that is, his old body, his old ways... And what if the family that board it are all the thoughts, feelings that live in the physical body, and the animals 'wild and tame' the passions that are natural to our physical lives? After the flood everything is calm and new. It is into a new world that Utnapishtim enters, a world even where the gods converse with him. His way of perceiving is new.

All of this, however, was not for Gilgamesh. Utnapishtim puts him to the test. But he is not able to stay awake for six days and seven nights. He has to return to his kingdom and rules successfully and gloriously for many years. But dies a man, a mortal. Permanence eluded him.

Chapter 8

Constructing the Boat

The name of the boat

One of the meanings of the word 'Islam' is submission, submission to the law, to the commandments of Allah as revealed through the Prophet Mohammed. The Koran consists of guidance in reconstructing life according to new rules. Noah (in the sura 11.36) is presented as the good man, the man who accepts monotheism when others don't. Rejecting polytheism and embracing monotheism is a form of reconstruction. Noah is told by Allah to construct a boat 'under Our eye and Our Revelation'. Under the supervision of Allah and following Allah's instructions therefore. He is instructed to take on board his family except a son ('Surely he is not of your family; verily his work is unrighteous, so ask not of me that of which you have no knowledge'), so only the worthy are to be taken. It is not clear what the criterion for worthiness might be and we are told not to ask – which suggests that it is not something as simple as following rites and observances. He is also to take male plus female of each kind. All others are to be destroyed. In sura 71 Noah tries to convince his people to change their ways: Allah will give them 'gardens and bestow on you rivers' – meaning they will go through death to paradise. Allah 'has brought you forth from the dust of the earth and afterwards he will return you to it and bring you forth again'. But this comes at a cost, just as Gilgamesh had to pay a cost by carrying out certain specific tasks to get to Utnapishtim. And this cost is the cost of a kind of 'reconstruction'. Abandoning the old body (the old ways) and taking on the new body (the new ways) will mean that the Book of Deeds, presented after death to the departed, will guarantee resurrection. The message has now become more explicit. But, as I have intimated above, the precise meaning of 'new body' and 'new ways' may not be as simple as mere adherence to rites.

Those who accept the Koran will accept that Allah 'has lodged us in a home that will last forever, where toil will not touch us, nor weariness will touch us'. 'Home' can only mean a new body, a spiritual body, non-physical, unaffected by time, or illness or fatigue.

And this new life in a new body is earned by following certain guidelines, just as Utnapishtim built his boat or as Gilgamesh cut trees and made poles (though *his* efforts did not have the same result…). These 'guidelines' for reconstruction may have to do with becoming aware of the permanent part of us, of the spiritual body within us. The secret is in getting to know how we can develop this awareness.

If we turn to the early books of the Old Testament we learn that men lived too long and were evil. So something was not quite right. We learn also that very definite instructions, with precise measurements, were given to Noah regarding the dimensions of the boat. Noah was to get into the boat 'with whole family' and male and female of all species. Change and upheaval were in the air. The only safe way through them was to construct… It seemed impossible to me not to see parallels with Gilgamesh and with the Koran.

And are there not echoes in the following words of the Sufi mystic, Jalal-Ud-Din Rumi?

When a tailor cuts up a cloth piece by piece,
Does anyone go up to him and strike him and say,
'Why have you torn up this beautiful satin;
What can I do with scraps of torn-up cloth?'
Each time that builders come to repair an old building
Don't they begin by destroying what was there before?
Look at the carpenter or the blacksmith or the butcher;

> With them too you will find that destruction precedes renewal.

Destruction followed by reconstruction. Flood followed by renewal. But best seen as an inner process.

The Upanishads are some of the oldest Hindu texts. They form part of the Vedas, that part that deals with the knowledge of God as opposed to rites and observances. It is not known how many Upanishads there were originally, but one hundred and eight have survived. We don't know who wrote them or when, at least with any accuracy. The oldest ones were probably composed around the eighth century before the Christian era. They are the basis of Hindu metaphysics.

In the Upanishads it is very simple: the soul and God are one. One of them is Brahman, the Universal Soul, and the other is Atman, the individual soul. The soul is not the ego, the personality, the soul is not ME: on the contrary I AM THAT (*Tat tvam asi*), I am one with everything that surrounds me…

When we study the Upanishads we see an exercise in reconstruction also, like the one related in the Epic of Gilgamesh. But reconstruction of a different kind. Or so it seems. But is it really so different? The ideal set in the Upanishads is to see the One, not to see everything separate and unconnected but to see that the Spirit or the Self is in all things. The *Chandogya* Upanishad: 'When one sees nothing but the One, knows nothing but the One – there is the Infinite. When one sees another, hears another, knows another – there is the finite.' And what is infinite, the Upanishad tells us, is immortal, whereas what is finite is mortal.

Curiously or not we can find the same thought in Saint Paul: 'For as the body is one, and hath many members, and all the members of that one body being many, are one body: so also is Christ.'

Gilgamesh, despite his efforts and his desires, remained a separate being. He was a man absorbed in his personality, in his basically selfish desires, a man who lost his temper easily. A man who, despite all his physical power, was not able to 'prevail against sleep for six days and seven nights', which Utnapishtim told him would help him find immortal life. Gilgamesh died a mortal, with only his reputation surviving, for a limited time. He had lived in the finite.

Sri Aurobindo, founder of the Pondichery ashram, in his commentary on the Upanishad *Isha*, dwells on the need for us to reconstruct ourselves, to move out of a perception of life and living which is imperfect and incomplete to a realization of our divine nature and of the divine nature of all that surrounds us. Even suffering and unhappiness contain, in a veiled form, *ananda* or beatitude. But to get behind the veil requires that we develop another consciousness, a consciousness of the Self. Says Aurobindo: '(the individual soul) has to acquire knowledge of the transcendental Self, and through this knowledge of unity, extend its conscious existence so as to embrace multiplicity.' Paul once more: 'It is the same God which worketh all in all.'

Things are in such a way that the individual sees himself/herself as distinct from God and also distinct from all other individuals. Thus there is the relative (seeing things as separate) and the absolute. The absolute is real, the rest is not. But that does not mean that the world is a fiction. What it does mean is that there is no creation, there is only 'becoming'. 'Becoming' is movement and movement – nature – is what we live in. This movement which is a creative force, uniting mind and matter, is called *maya*. But movement is impermanent. So in that sense it lacks reality. But this movement is necessary; it permits the Creator to stand aside and observe the relative.

'The Self is one. Unmoving, it moves swifter than thought. The senses do not overtake it, for always it goes before. Remaining still it outstrips all that runs.' Without the Self there is no life. The Self is one with the Creator; because it moves and yet doesn't move it contains all that moves and all that doesn't move.

'To the ignorant the Self appears to move – yet it moves not. From the ignorant it is far distant – yet it is near. It is within all and it is without all.' (*Isha* Upanishad) If the Creator did not contain all and allow these opposites of absolute and relative, that which is relative would disintegrate into the absolute, as into a Black Hole. But that which is relative MUST exist for to have only the absolute would be meaningless (for us human beings).

So the Self which is Brahman, God, is in all things both those permanent and those impermanent. Everything already exists in Brahman. All that moves – where 'all' here means all the elements of becoming, everything that is impermanent – is simply the realization of what is already in Brahman. Beyond time, Brahman contains the present, the past and the future. Everything is already in Brahman before it can come into being in the world.

If we follow the thinking of the Upanishads we find that the Self gradually reveals itself to the individual consciousness – over a series of incarnations – and that individual consciousness progressively becomes more and more aware of the Unity of all being. And this consciousness of the Self has its beginning at the highest spiritual level of our being and gradually descends into our thoughts, our feelings and our physical being. Usually we are conscious only of our existence in the physical, emotional and intellectual levels. It is the interplay of these levels, the struggle between opposites, the conflicts, the love and hate, attraction and repulsion, that makes up the reality of our day-to-day lives. But Hinduism, and Hinduism is not alone in this, teaches that we have other levels that we are not conscious of. *Chit* is the term given to the Absolute, which contains multiplicity and unity and is itself composed of seven levels. In the supra-conscious levels of *chit* we find *Sat*, the essence of our being, in its infinite and indivisible nature, in contrast to the being that is constantly changing and transforming itself. We find also *Ananda*, which is beatitude, felicity beyond senses and emotions which for their part are at the mercy of physical contacts and therefore changing and impermanent.

This may seem a very laborious and not always transparently clear way of approaching the conception of soul in the Upanishads. But the idea that right down to our physical being we will gradually become conscious of the Self, of God, is surely the same thing as the Spiritual Body that Saint Paul spoke of and which we saw in the story of the Ark in Gilgamesh. Saint Paul writes: '(…) we shall be changed. For this corruptible must put on incorruption, and this mortal must put on immortality.' He makes clear earlier that resurrection is in a spiritual body ('There is a natural body and there is a spiritual body').

'Corruptible' is what rots, what is made of imperfect material, 'mortal' is likewise that which carries death within it. It is impossible not to see the parallels with the philosophy of the Upanishads.

In the *Svetesvatara* Upanishad we can find something much more explicit:

'The truth is that you are always united with the Lord, but you must *know* this (…)' Fire, though present in the firesticks, is not perceived until one stick is rubbed against another. Our Self is like that fire and can be awakened by meditation. 'Thus shall you realize God, who is hidden within the body as fire is hidden in the wood.'

The aim of life, say the Upanishads, is to become conscious of those higher levels, to come to live with the Self, the Unity and its permanence. This takes us away from the imperfect soul or self that we are usually conscious of, to a vaster consciousness and to immortality, which is the purpose of our existence. Thus, in our physical bodies we become fully aware of Unity. In the words of Paul we come into our spiritual body. In it we are aware of both unity and multiplicity, we are living in the world, able to reconcile impermanence and permanence. We find love for all things and all beings. Suffering and pain become aspects of the Divine, we are above attraction and repulsion.

Immortality is the death of the limited ego leading to the consciousness of the vaster ego that is the Self. The soul is then able to see its successive life experiences in the course of its different past lives, it is then free from birth and death, from the chain of cause and effect, from the pull of attraction and repulsion.

The Christian Communion has already been mentioned. The instructions given by Christ at the Last Supper are usually thought to be new but it is more than possible to see parallels with the much older teaching of the Upanishads, as exemplified in the *Isha* and *Chandogya* Upanishads. Communion is the search for unity, unity with all beings and unity with God. There are two beings in Jesus Christ. There is the one who hesitated, showed weakness in Gethsemane ('Father, if thou be willing remove this cup from me') but there is the other who accepts God's will ('Nevertheless, not my will but thine be done'). The weaker, more human being comes back on the Cross when in his suffering Jesus cries out, 'Eloi, Eloi, lama sabachtani?' (Oh my God, why have you forsaken me?) We can see the human side, the impermanent, the changing, and the permanent side, the divine side, which is in union with God, with the All, with the Self in Hindu terms. When Jesus says on the cross, 'Forgive them, Lord, for they know not what to do', it is the God-element in Him that is speaking; the purely human, changeable element would be incapable of this forgiveness.

The Christian Communion represents Unity within multiplicity as in *Isha*. Partaking of the bread and the wine is partaking of the Self; it is being one with the All, passing out of the impermanent into the changeless.

Saint John is the Christian evangelist who reveals most about the underlying thinking of Christianity and who has marked the development of Christian thinking. It is worth highlighting a few of the key statements that Jesus made in his last exchanges with his disciples as related by John.

'In the world ye shall have tribulation, but be of good cheer; I have overcome the world.'

'For all that is in the world, the lust of the flesh and the lust of the eyes, and the pride of life, is not of the Father, but is of the world. And the world passeth away, and the lust thereof; but he that doeth the will of God abideth forever.' A summary of the nature of impermanence and permanence...

'And the Glory which thou givest me I have given them (the disciples); that they may be one, even as we are one: I in them and thou in me, that they may be made perfect in one.'

The Upanishad Kaivalya says something very close to this: 'From me all emerge, and to me all return. I am Brahman – One without a second.'

The story of Jesus is the story of reaching that higher spirit in us which transcends time and place, which is beyond suffering, beyond pleasure.

The Upanishad *Chandogya,* already mentioned, describes how the Self can rise above pleasure and pain by loosening the association with the body. 'Rising above physical consciousness, knowing the Self to be distinct from the mind and the body, knowing it in its true light, one rejoices and is free'.

Are there any better words than those to describe the Passion?

In the Gospel of John: 'Verily, verily, I say unto you, he that believeth on me shall have everlasting life. I am that bread of life. Your fathers did eat manna in the wilderness and are dead. This is the bread that cometh down from heaven, that a man may eat thereof and not die.' Manna, though it appeared miraculously to the people of Israel who were travelling with Moses, was bread of a physical kind but the 'bread that cometh down from heaven' cannot be physical bread, it has to be spiritual. Just as the everlasting life which it gives is also spiritual.

But having attained even this higher state does not mean that one renounces life. One has to live in the world however impermanent and changing it may be: 'I pray not that thou shouldest take them out of the world, but that thou shouldest keep them from the evil. ... As thou hast sent me into the world, even so have I also sent them into the world.' (Jesus Christ as reported by John.)

'To darkness are they doomed who devote themselves only to life in the world, and to a greater darkness they who devote themselves only to meditation.' The Upanishad *Isha*.

More than Hinduism, Buddhism is commonly seen as a religion of ethics, of how to behave. The Noble Eightfold Path explains to people how they should conduct their lives if they wish to attain 'liberation' from the cycle of death and rebirth which is the aim of the devout Buddhist. The material world we live in is characterized by three things, old age, disease and death. No one can ever escape these except by annihilating the ego and attaining liberation, which the Buddhists call *nirvana*, and which implies escape from the need to be reborn in this world which is the world of suffering. The first step, and the most difficult one, towards annihilating the ego is to eliminate craving. Craving leads to attachment, leading to actions which lead to continued rebirth in the material world. Craving is controlled by the mind through meditation. Meditation leads to detachment from the senses and this cessation of dependence on the senses leads to cessation of contact, which leads to cession of feeling, which leads to cessation of craving.

Karma is the force that rules the world, that links past, present and future. It is a simple system of cause and effect, but in Buddhism, as in Hinduism, it is what permits and sustains life. You reap what you sow. Every action, every thought and feeling even is a cause which will produce an effect at some time in the future. Effects are unavoidable. There is no place for the Christian concept of Redemption, of forgiveness of sins; everything must be paid for or rewarded as the case may be. You can create good karma or you can create bad karma, it's up to you. It is all very mechanical. The theory of Karma makes the idea of a soul superfluous. And for this reason Buddhists are thought to have no belief in a soul that survives death. The Buddha is thought to have discouraged discussion of such metaphysical subjects. Once in a forest he was asked about these things by a disciple. He is said to have scooped up a handful of leaves from the forest floor and to have said: 'What I teach you is like the amount of leaves in my hand, what there is to know is like all the leaves in the forest.'

Every known major religion has a popular teaching available to everyone, an 'exoteric' teaching, and also a more secret 'esoteric' teaching reserved for the few. The Cabbala in Judaism or Sufism in Islam. Though Sufism is not alone in Islam. Averroes freely admitted that there were simple ideas that were suitable for the masses whereas the philosopher was allowed more advanced interpretations, interpretations that could even be dangerous for the masses. The Mysteries of ancient Egypt, of Greece and even Rome were also esoteric teachings reserved for an elite. The esoteric element of Christianity is not immediately perceivable, if at all. But it is reasonable to think that an esoteric teaching existed. Otherwise how could one explain that such a powerful movement had as a basis such a threadbare story? Even when we look at the four gospels (which were not written immediately after the death of Jesus) we have essentially the same short story four times. When one looks at the esoteric side of Buddhism things become less simple than they appear in popular belief. There is the Buddhist prayer or meditation theme – mentioned in a previous chapter – which goes like this:

> (Thinking of the body): This is not mine, this am I not, this is not my soul.
> (Thinking of the feelings): These are not mine, these am I not, these are not my soul.
> (Thinking of my thoughts): These are not mine, these am I not, these are not my soul.

> (Thinking of my mental states): These are not mine, these am I not, these are not my soul.
> (Thinking of my ego): This is not mine, this am I not, this is not my soul.

Those elements, body, feelings, thoughts, mental states are the impermanent, perishable parts of us. In the long term they are of no consequence. When one succeeds in living beyond these, one gets closer to the more permanent parts of our being, to our 'higher bodies' in Buddhist and Hindu terms. And it is in these higher bodies that you find the soul. The distinction between personality and individuality is a useful one that helps understand these beliefs. A writer and expert on Buddhism wrote:

> The successive appearances (...) of a certain being are a succession of personalities. In each birth the personality differs from that of the previous or next succeeding birth. Karma, the deus ex machina, masks itself now in the personality of a sage, again as an artisan, and so on throughout the string of births. But although the personalities ever shift, the one line of life along which they are strung like a row of beads remains unbroken. It is ever that particular line, never any other. It is therefore individual; (...) The denial of soul by the Buddha points to the prevalent, delusive belief in an independent transmissible personality.
> (A.P. Sinnett: Esoteric Buddhism)

What is transmitted, therefore, is the individuality not the personality or what we commonly call the 'ego', which brings us back to the notion of Self and of the spiritual body of Saint Paul, and the immortal body of Utnapishtim. At the end of the day, the esoteric teaching of Buddhism tells us, we would be able to look back on a string of different personalities, but in fact all of that will have little interest for us; they will seem distant and trivial, roles we played that are no longer relevant, no longer important. What was important was how successfully we solved the problems we were faced with, how much we were able to apprehend the Self and Unity.

'All the world's a stage and all the men and women merely players: they have their exits and their entrances; and one man in his time plays many parts.' (W. Shakespeare, *As You Like It)*

To return to the Koran, when Noah is told to embark on the boat built under careful supervision it is clear that there is a question of change. From something imperfect to something better. To those who change the Lord will give gardens and 'bestow rivers'. Some interpret this as meaning a new sensitivity is born in the body, an awakening of the *chakras,* the centres of energy. Those who change will find a 'home' where there is no toil and no weariness. Is this not the same as being born in the spiritual body, the permanent Self, the individuality? It remains to render more explicit what is meant by being worthy enough to embark on the boat, and therefore what the term 'submission' or 'Islam' may entail. Submission to the higher Self, to the divine part of our nature, the 'home that will last forever' which Allah has lodged within us?

If there is such a thing as immortality and if that condition is substantially different from what we are living now, it is obvious that some sort of preparation or briefing would be welcome. It is not immediately obvious that the established religions help in these matters, that is, in knowing the nature of immortality and knowing how to be ready for it. And yet I would argue strongly that the guidelines are there just as the instructions to Utnapishtim about how to build his boat.

And this is where we come to the role of ethics and behaviour: the Commandments, the five tenets of Islam, the Noble Eightfold path, the Talmud etc. Those are all guidelines for living correctly in society, and certainly that is important. But there is something more. There is the suggestion that attention to certain guidelines, which often seem constraining and a limit on our freedom, can lead to an awareness of the permanent Self. How can this be so, indeed can it be so? And what exactly are those guidelines? Talking of one hundred and twenty poles, of staying awake for a week, of realizing the Inner Self is fine but not helpful in practical terms. This is a subject which the following chapter begins to examine.

But first, and to end this chapter, it is worth looking at what Hindu thinking terms 'discrimination'.

The Upanishad *Mundaka* tells us that we cannot see the Inner Self or express the Inner self in words, that we cannot perceive the Inner Self with our five senses, cannot reach it by ritual or by fast but, 'when through discrimination the heart has become pure, then, in meditation, the Impersonal Self is revealed'.

At every moment of our lives we can make a choice, we can discriminate between one action and another. Behind the precepts of our established religions lies the reality of choice. And in this way we exercise our free will. But what is it that enables us to make choices in our best interests, and what are our best interests? This is where this concept of discrimination has to be important. And also the criteria that allow us to apply discrimination. The concept and the criteria together would allow us to apprehend the Self, the Permanent in us, the part that does not die with the flesh. Hinduism, as we shall see in the next chapter, is not the only religion to advocate discrimination and by looking at examples of discrimination it might be possible to get closer to reaching what I have termed our 'individuality'. And if 'individuality' is the name of the boat, it is discrimination that would allow us to select the appropriate materials to construct it.

Chapter 9

Choosing the Materials

Learning to discriminate

'When through discrimination the heart has been made pure', says the Upanishad *Mundaka*, 'then, in meditation, the Impersonal Self is revealed.' And this can allow man to perceive the Eternal Self and so be able to live in death. (The Eternal Self and the human Soul are the same, for the Hindu.) There is much that is not clear here. Even if we accept that the 'Eternal Self' is the Impersonal Self and is the same as the individuality (as discussed in chapter 6 and chapter 8) what is it that can help us 'live in death'? More to the point, what does it mean to live in death? HOW can we LIVE in DEATH? This means having some kind of 'body' (which has to be non-physical and indestructible) with faculties of perception of some sort. Either we possess this body already, and are unaware of that, or we must acquire it, construct it. If we have to construct this personal and permanent Self in order to pass through death then how do we do that? And what is the nature of this self, how does one recognize it? The metaphor of the boat is a useful one. We have to construct the vehicle which will carry us through death. To do this we have to find and select materials. And this reconstruction will lead to a new way of perceiving a new reality. But how do we go about this selection of materials?

As was pointed out at the end of the last chapter we are constantly making choices in life. Some of these choices are trivial; others are not. On some of these choices our spiritual welfare depends. The Koran constantly says that although evidence and signs are put before mankind many choose to ignore them. It is the Koran itself, in Islam, which allows men to discriminate between what is good and what is bad. The Koran continually stresses 'understanding the signs' (*ayât* = signs, lessons, evidence, etc). It says: 'And indeed we have put forth every kind of example in this Koran, for mankind. But man is ever more quarrelsome than anything'. Several times the Koran talks about 'criteria for right and wrong' and in Sura 45.15 we find: 'Whosoever does a good deed it is for his own self; and whosoever does evil, it is against his own self'. So choosing to do a good deed is a way of constructing one's 'own self'. And doing 'evil' is destructive of one's 'own self'.

Similar lessons or guidance can be found in the Old Testament and the New. Lucifer chose, Adam and Eve made a choice, Abraham chose, the disciples chose to follow Jesus, Judas chose. And all of these choices had effects. Many of the parables in the New Testament illustrate the consequences of one *choice* or another. The problem is that there are times when we face a choice which seems to be a 50/50 choice but in fact the balance is weighted to one side and sadly for us that side is often not the better one. Through an inherent laziness and despite a small dissenting voice within us we sometimes select the option that seems easier, or more immediately rewarding, or more fun than an alternative which would be better in the long run – and we are often even partly conscious of that.

Buddhism, while inheriting much of the metaphysics of Hinduism (perhaps all Buddhists might not agree with this assertion), has greatly developed the understanding of psychological processes. The Dhammapada begins: 'Mind is the forerunner of all evil states. Mind is chief; mind-made are they. If one speaks or acts with a wicked mind, because of that, suffering follows one, even as the wheel follows the hoof of the draught-ox.' And of course if one speaks and acts with a pure mind 'happiness follows one, even as one's shadow that never leaves'.

As we saw earlier, in the Hindu tradition, the Upanishad *Mundaka* says that when the heart is made pure through discrimination, 'the Impersonal Self is revealed'. The meaning of 'purity' needs clarification, as well as the meaning of 'heart'. The heart is seen as the seat of consciousness in Hindu philosophy, and this is generally accepted in Buddhist thinking also. Purity is the 'mental state of wisdom' (the term comes from Narada, *The Manual of Abhidhamma*) which permits you to see things as they really are: that there is nothing permanent in matter and that mind changes even faster than matter! Everything we do and know NOW is intimately bound up with the physical world and therefore with what is impermanent. Understanding the true nature of this impermanence is the result of the heart being purified. But lack of this purity of heart is the greatest problem we face, says Buddhism. You can find in Buddhism very detailed explanations of physics and psychology though the terms used are very different from those used in modern science. The *Abhidhamma* is the philosophy of Buddhism. All is change, it tells us, all conditioned things are subject to change. 'Our ego-personality is nothing more than a mere composition of mind and matter – the former consisting of fleeting mental states that arise as a result of the senses coming into contact with the sense-stimuli, and the latter of forces and qualities that manifest themselves in multifarious phenomena.' Buddhist philosophy gives us an analysis of the stages our thought processes go through when we perceive the world around us, an analysis that highlights the transitory nature of each fleeting moment. All of us, at times in our lives, pause to think about how quickly things pass away, how each present moment is inexorably swept into the past, and how each present moment is not only immeasurably brief but infinitesimally small, part of ourselves only in the vastness of the universe. Buddhist psychology tackles the problem in a direct and illuminating way. It gives the example of our perception of objects, events etc. Perceiving any material thing we go through a series of 'thought-moments', each of which is infinitely short in time, so short that we are not conscious of them. Before perception our mind is in a state of what might be called unconscious-consciousness. This state is disturbed by the new phenomenon – that is the first thought-moment. The next thought moment is the realization that something is there. Then comes sight of the object (eye consciousness, seeing the object and no more), then identifying the object (investigating consciousness), then determining the relevance or value of the object (determining consciousness – discrimination), and then action ethical or not (which engenders karma). All of this happens in an infinitely short period of time and our lives are made of such thought-moments and thought-processes embedded in periods of 'unconscious-consciousness' (the Sanskrit term *bhavanga* is apparently very hard to translate; this is an attempt to paraphrase the meaning). In fact what I have described in terms of thought-moments is not complete: there are more than I have mentioned in this illustration. What Buddhism captures here is that our life is made up of millions (no, trillions upon trillions) of evanescent, split-split-second thought-moments that are our only reality. And each thought-moment is our only reality ONLY for as long as it lasts... In considering all of this we have to remember three key things. The first one is that the mind can be our friend and the mind can be our enemy. (In the Bhagavad-Gita Krishna tells Arjuna: 'Thy soul can be thy friend and thy soul can be thine enemy.') Awareness of the reality of thought-moments leads to greater attention to the fleeting present moment and greater awareness of impermanence. Such awareness is impossible if our mind is constantly distracted. The second key thing is that one of the thought-moments is 'determining consciousness' which determines the relevance or value of our perceived object (or action or mental state). This is the moment of DISCRIMINATION. And if we are to interpret in a meaningful way the Upanishad quoted at the beginning of the chapter, this is the moment when perception links to moral values (to the Noble Eightfold Path,[1] in Buddhism) and is crucial in our development as moral or immoral beings. And the third key point is that the thought-moment following this is the moment for action, which may be good or bad, and which will determine karma: it is the cause which will produce effects.

The doctrine of *karma* has been widely explained and commented on in our day and it is hardly necessary to explain it again. One or two points though are important with regard to the topic of this chapter. *Karma* is the law that governs cause and effect. We reap what we sow and we may reap it in this life or in the next or in a future existence at any time. It is a law unto itself and totally independent of all else. It is automatic, mechanical; it is transmitted from one existence to another. And it concerns not only actions, but words and thoughts. *Karma* exists in Hinduism of course but it is in Buddhism that it is absolutely central: there is no God (mentioned) in Buddhism, no angels, no Brahman or Atman, there is only *karma.* And so discrimination exercised by the individual is the only source of his or her salvation. We will get help from no other source but ourselves.

When we look at how Buddhism treats death we find some important differences with Hinduism and with the kind of Buddhism exemplified by The Tibetan Book of the Dead. For one thing Theravada Buddhists (the Buddhists of Sri Lanka and Thailand for example) seem to take reincarnation as being fairly immediate after death. And also, more importantly, there is no room for the concept of a personal soul. Since everything is in constant flux and all is subject to decay, everything that is human disappears and decays, including any mental elements. Death is 'a temporary end to a temporary phenomenon'. But the energies that were the person alive are reconstituted in a new existence so there is a continuity of process. A particular passage in Narada's book is striking:

> The passing away of the consciousness of the past birth is the occasion for the arising of the new consciousness in a subse-

> quent birth. However nothing unchangeable or permanent is transmitted from the past to the present.
>
> Just as the wheel rests on the ground only at one point, so, strictly speaking, we live for only one thought-moment. We are always in the present, and that present is ever slipping into the irrevocable past. Each momentary consciousness of this ever-changing life-process, on passing away, transmits its whole energy, and the indelibly recorded impressions on it, to its successor. Each fresh consciousness, therefore, consists of the potentiality of its predecessors together with something more. At death the consciousness perishes, as in truth it perishes every moment, only to give birth to another in a rebirth. This renewed consciousness inherits all its past experiences.

The last sentence is surely very significant. Another image that Narada uses is that of transmitting light from one source, a candle for example, to another. Light is transmitted but it is not the same light. (It is still light.)

There is something here that comes close to the notions of personality and individuality outlined in previous chapters. Close but there is much more meat, much more depth in the Buddhist explanation. Buddhist philosophy is nothing if not exhaustive and detailed. Going deeper into Buddhist thinking one finds that there is a category of particularly spiritually developed human beings, for example *Arahants* (who have reached enlightenment and who do not need to be reborn) or *bodhisattvas* (potential Buddhas who accept reincarnation to help others). All mankind can evolve into these spheres. Evolving into these spheres must entail having the right vehicle. This can be seen as the creation over many existences of a higher and more subtle body and that this thinking therefore joins what was said about Utnapishtim and his boat, about Saint Paul's 'spiritual body', and Averroes' assertion that resurrection cannot be in physical body.

How does this help us construct a personal and permanent Self which can be our vehicle in passing through death? The question is still without an answer. In Buddhism the answer, we are told, is to be aware of the Four Noble Truths and the Noble Eightfold Path (see above), to practise meditation on the impermanence of all things, to understand craving in all its forms and to eradicate the ego. Our problem, says Buddhism, is that we do not see things as they really are. Quite right when you think of what modern physics and quantum mechanics have to say!

'When through discrimination the heart has become pure...' The chapter began with that thought. 'Purity' meant a clarity of vision, and the heart is the seat of consciousness. So to attain this 'mental state of wisdom' we would need to work on our consciousness, through discrimination, to get it away from attaching importance to what is not permanent – and develop or hone the resulting new perception. This seemed to be a starting point towards finding the answer to that question of constructing or finding some permanent self. The sub-title of this chapter is 'Learning to discriminate'. The chapter has emphasized the role of the consciousness of each passing moment and of choice and how these factors influence our development as human and spiritual beings. And underlying these considerations has been the idea that it is possible to develop other awarenesses and that doing so will help us understand and pass through the experience of death. The experiences of mystics have often spoken of things outside the realms of our ordinary physical and psychic existence. The next chapter will try to connect with several mystics.

Chapter 10

Jalal-Ud-Din, Teresa and Juan

What do two Spaniards and an Afghan have in common?

Northern Europe in the 16th century was in the turmoil of religious change with the spread of Protestantism. Spain, sheltered by the Pyrenees, was spared most of this but there was reform there as well of an internal kind. Juan de Yepes y Alvarez and Teresa de Cepeda y Hamada (to give them their full names) met somewhere in the middle of the 16th century in central Spain. They were very different personalities. From Teresa's autobiography we get the impression of an outgoing, vibrant, strong-willed individual who was used to getting her own way. A kind of 16th century Mother Teresa of Calcutta, perhaps, in character anyway. He, on the other hand, seems to have been of a more retiring nature, shy almost. The century they lived in was the century of the birth of Protestantism and of the Reform. Although the protestant fever did not affect Spain to the degree that it affected northern Europe and even France, nonetheless both Teresa and John felt deeply the need for change and became active in a reform of the Carmelite order and that occupied most of their religious lives.

But there was something else that united these two very different personalities. They were both mystics. They both lived mystical ecstatic experiences which they saw as 'union with God'. And they both wrote about it. And both were criticized by certain members of the Church who saw their experiences as the work of the devil. But at the end of the day they won. She was to become known as Saint Teresa of Avila and he, Saint John of the Cross.

Teresa certainly seems to have been something of a character.

In those days before the reform of the Order the nuns were free to receive visitors and Teresa relates how she liked to spend hours chattering idly with them. In her autobiography she tells us how for many years she had to struggle between the opposites of prayer and life in the world, how she failed God (as she puts it) time and time again, how she did not care for minor sins, did not fear mortal sins as she should have, and did not put distance 'between herself and the dangers'. This struggle, when she enjoyed 'neither God nor the world', lasted for some eighteen years. But she was eventually able to withdraw from the 'vanities of the world', as she put it, and from then on everything became easy. She wrote: 'The Holy Spirit like a powerful hurricane will propel the small ship of our soul over more distance towards saintliness than we ourselves would achieve in months and years of our own efforts.' What Christians term the grace of God, it seems, was a key factor in her case.

And presumably in the case of John of the Cross also. He has left a number of powerful and beautiful mystical poems. They describe the ineffable joy of mystical experience and the anguish of being cut off from it. What is probably his best known poem *En una noche oscura* (*Upon a gloomy night*) uses the symbolism of the dark night to relate how he enters into meditation or prayer:

In, safety, in disguise,
In darkness up the secret stair I crept
(Oh happy enterprise)
Concealed from other eyes
When all the house at length in silence slept.

And through this escape into the present moment he reaches a state of mystical union with the God or the Self:

Within my flowering breast
Which only for himself entire I save

He sank into his rest
And all my gifts I gave
Lulled by the airs with which the cedars wave.

In another poem he captures, I found, the going-beyond-intellect which is what mystics of other traditions have drawn attention to:

I entered in, I know not where,
And I remained, though knowing naught,
Transcending knowledge with my thought.

This recalls the Upanishad Svetasvatara: 'Meditate upon pure consciousness as distinct from the ordinary consciousness.' Or Brihadaranyaka: 'He who dwells in the mind but is separate from the mind, whom the mind does not know ... is the Inner Ruler, the Immortal.' There is less overt Christian imagery in John than in Teresa and it seems Catholic authorities have sometimes had difficulty adapting his mysticism to orthodoxy. Like Teresa he was attacked in his days by conventional Carmelites and others and even spent some eight months in prison.

What can be learnt from these two Spanish mystics about how to obtain that elusive purity of knowledge spoken of in the last chapter (p. 85)?

They were very different, that has been said, so personality does not seem to be a factor. Both emphasize that 'the way is long and arduous', that persistence is necessary and disregard for what others think (otherwise they would not have risked opprobrium and even prison). Both remained active in the world yet for each the experience of mystical union was as necessary as a drug to an addict. Saint John of the Cross describes the experience of lack vividly:

I live without inhabiting

Myself – in such a wise that I
Am dying that I do not die.

So dying to a part of oneself is a prerequisite for the experience. What is this part that must die? Teresa who was an extrovert and had a strong personality, from what we can gather, was for many years taken up with things of the world and only later reached an awareness of the 'vanity of the world'. It was only then that she began through prayer and meditation to have her mystical experiences. Also she tells us also that she felt herself 'base', which I take to mean 'unworthy' or 'inferior'. Indications, perhaps, that she was diminishing the importance not necessarily of her personality, but of the selfish demands of her personality, the desire for personal gratification. John was already a retiring and shy person so in his case a detachment from the pleasures or trivia of the world was easier. But, and there seems to be a paradox here, though leading lives of prayer and meditation, both these saints were very active in the world… Ah, but of course they were not working for themselves, or for their own pleasure or satisfaction. It is, however, notoriously difficult to be sure that even when you believe you are working for God you are not really giving satisfaction to yourself. A look at some mystics from other traditions could help throw light on the issue and outside Christianity and the traditions of the Indian subcontinent the Sufis are an obvious choice.

But we cannot leave these two Christian mystics without a mention of the sexual symbolism that can be found in their descriptions especially in those of John of the Cross. Freudian psychologists could without a doubt say a lot about these. But it is also possible to relate it to the erotic statues of Hindu origin, the statues of Khajurabo for example. This use of the profane, of profane love, to represent a religious experience says several things. It says that there is a similarity between sexual pleasure and mystical union. (I recall hearing an eastern Master telling her audience that the experience of beatitude or ecstasy was similar to an orgasm.) It also says and very importantly that the human soul is amorous (few express this better than Saint John of the Cross and Jalal-Ud-Din Rumi – see below). But there is a difference. In Hinduism there is no taboo on sex but logically, in the Hindu system of values, it has to be seen as a source of attachment to the world, to the physical and therefore to the impermanent, to what is doomed to pass away. The erotic carvings therefore represent the Permanent through allusion to the impermanent. The Unknown through the known.

Jalal-Ud-Din Rumi, the 13th century Sufi poet from Persia, born in Balk in Afghanistan, was a mystic also and his very direct, deceptively simple language has captured the imagination of many people of different faiths. He lived, it would seem, with a permanent mystical vision of the Oneness of all. He suffered bereavement, like Gilgamesh, at the loss of a close friend but found the solution to his grief in the realization that all is one, that his friend was always with him:

> Why should I seek? I am the same as
> He. His essence speaks through me
> I have been looking for myself.

Like John of the Cross, Rumi uses the language of lovers. The Beloved, in Rumi's poems, is the Self, the primal source, with which we seek union; it is the 'always-so' of the Tao (see the next chapter). To reach it one must exercise discrimination. One of his poems is entitled 'Taste with Discrimination'. It tells of different kinds of wine. They will all make you drunk but only one 'wins the house that no one will want to leave':

> Oh connoisseur of wine, take care, taste with discrimination
> So you find a wine that hasn't been adulterated.

To be able to exercise this discrimination sacrifice is required. And Rumi is very direct here: he is talking of sacrifice of the self: 'The path towards God is the sacrifice of the self.'

And this sacrifice of the self cannot be achieved without suffering for on this path 'in every thicket lurks a danger to make a person whose soul is as fragile as a flask of glass turn back and retrace his steps'. And, just as Teresa and John wrote, the way is not only hard but long, and dying to oneself is much more difficult than we imagine it to be:

> You've endured many terrible griefs
> But you're still under a veil –
> Because dying to yourself
> Is the fundamental principle
> And you haven't adhered to it.

Destruction precedes renewal, says Rumi in another poem and in his direct, inimitable style – a medieval Robert Frost, stating the obvious but with a deeper layer of meaning. For a new life to begin, an old one must die, for a new self to be realized, the old one must disappear. 'The only condition for experiencing resurrection,' he says in another poem appropriately entitled Resurrection, 'is to die first.'

> How can we win authentic awareness?
> By renouncing knowledge.
> How can we seek salvation?
> By renouncing personal salvation.
> How can we look for existence?
> By renouncing our existence.

The purity of knowledge lies in renouncing intellectual knowledge, in forgetting about personal salvation, and in striving towards non-existence. This brings us back to the

Cabbala and particularly to the concepts of *Ain Soph Aur, Ain Soph* and *Ain* (see chapter 3, page 31; chapter 4, page 44). We are beyond Creation at this level, beyond angels and archangels, into pure emptiness, pure mystery, but indestructible now.

Love is a theme that comes back again and again in the poems of Jalal-Ud-Din Rumi. Only the heart counts:

> Turn to the heart and go forward, travellers of the night,
> That's where you will find trees and streams of living water.

Reading through Rumi's work it is clear that this divine love is in no way connected to the intellect and in no way a part of the personality. It is, in fact, linked to the permanent Self and to resurrection.

How do we start to construct this permanent Self, where we will find 'trees and streams of living water', where we attain 'authentic awareness' in non-existence? How do we attain to the purity of knowledge that seems to be a prerequisite if we accept what we find in Hinduism, Buddhism and in the Christian and Moslem mystics? In the section on Buddhist psychology above there was the notion of a given thought-moment which was the moment for ACTION and it followed the thought-moment of DISCRIMINATION. It could be worth the time to dig deeper into the concept of personality. For Buddhist psychology the personality is no more that a succession of fleeting mental states none of them of any permanence. We might see how this view compares with the standard western theories. In Freudian theory we start with our Id which is the basic urges; around the age of three we develop our Ego and from age 5 our Superego. The Id is based on the pleasure principle – it just sees what feels good and does it without regard to the situation or results. When the Ego develops however the individual understands that there are other people who are different from ourselves and the consequences of our actions may affect them. With the development of the Superego the individual develops a moral guide. So, in Freudian psychology DISCRIMINATION is the struggle of the Ego between the wishes of the Id and the 'advice' of the Superego. There is no contradiction with eastern thinking insofar as we can see the thought-moment where discrimination takes place as the struggle between Superego and Id with a resultant action which leads to *karma*. But it could be said that the Buddhist model goes a bit further. It sees all of these processes as part of the eternity of time and as a succession of fleeting moments that, each and every one of them, disappear forever. The western model does not mention permanence or its opposite. Or the role of the moment of discrimination in shaping action and consequence. Important features, pragmatically speaking. But both traditions share the idea of some 'moral' force playing a role in the personality: the superego is one way of putting it, discrimination followed by action followed by *karma* is the other. And though the possibility of choice is common to both, in both cases it is not the case that choices are easy: in one case it depends on the strength of the superego, and in the other being able to see things as they really are in the present moment.

Looking again at the Buddhist representation of death we find that great importance is put on the nature of the dying person's last thought-moment. This is the last instance of discrimination in his or her life. And it should happen in a state of purity of knowledge, of seeing things as they really are in the present moment. On the moral quality of this thought-moment the conditions of a subsequent life are determined – it is perhaps recollection of a good action, formulation of a good wish, an expression of selfless love and so on, or their opposites. For 'death is not the complete annihilation of a being, for though a particular life-span ends, the force which hitherto actuated it is not destroyed' (Narada). It is clear that the 'personality' (made up of a succession of fleeting thought-moments) IS destroyed. But the results of its actions are not destroyed. In Buddhism, a *jhana* is a developed state of consciousness acquired by meditation. Those who have cultivated the *jhanas* are born on the higher planes of varying levels of happiness and beauty. So while the unreal personality that we knew on earth does not survive it is possible to build up, through the *jhanas,* an ability to live as a different being. Back to Utnapishtim and his boat?

With regard to 'seeing things as they really are' Hinduism talks of *vidya* and *avidya*. *Vidya* is knowledge and *avidya* is ignorance. And the knowledge is that everything is one, not only connected but ONE, and not the series of separate things that we think we see. *Vidya* is unity, *avidya* is diversity.

In a book by Sri Aurobindo, the 20th century Hindu mystic and thinker who was co-founder of the ashram in Pondichery you will find him explaining how we have two souls, or, as he puts it, a double-soul.

> We have two mental faculties, on the one hand the surface mental faculty of our ego that has developed from birth and continues to develop, a superficial faculty created by us in the course of our emergence from Matter; on the other hand a subliminal mental faculty which is not handicapped by our current mental life and its limitations, something extensive, powerful, luminous, the true mental being behind what we mistakenly take for ourselves. In the same way we lead two lives, one in the external world, bound to our physical body (…) which lives, which is born and will die, the other a subliminal life-force which is not confined to the narrow space traced by our birth and our physical death, but which is our true vital being behind the form of life which in our ignorance we take for real.
> (Sri Aurobindo: The Life Divine)

Let's recall that 'purity of knowledge' can mean 'seeing things as they really are', and that means seeing things with our real soul, the one Sri Aurobindo is referring to in the passage just quoted. In his book *Life after Death,* Deepak Chopra puts the following words into the mouth of a fictional character:

> When you are happy, go deeply within yourself and become conscious of the person who experiences this happiness. When you are sad, go deeply within yourself and become conscious of the person experiencing this sadness. They are the same person. There is a tiny centre, motionless, which observes everything, which is a witness to everything. Become that motionless centre as often as you can. Pay attention to it, do not ignore it. Let it become familiar to you, it is your greatest ally. (...) At first this tiny, motionless centre will seem insignificant to you. Yet it can grow in size to infinity. When you die and have nothing to hold on to, [this centre] will fill the whole universe. The wise have repeated this truth time and time again, all through history.

In all that has been said above it was clear that self with a small initial letter meant the personality and that Self with a capital letter referred to the Soul, to the immortal in us. In the Psalms we find:

> Ye are gods and all of you are children of the most High.
> But ye shall die like men and fall like one of the princes.

What is man in us dies, what is god survives. But if we are to die to the personality, what does this mean in practical terms? In everyday terms, aside from what psychology says, we understand our personality to be.... what? Our character, how we control or manifest our feelings, how we relate to and influence others, our likes and dislikes (whether we like music, what kind of music, what kind of people we get on with), our pleasures, (family and friends, sport and so on). Can we easily reject all of this? It seems to me that we cannot and should not. But what we can and what we should do is to realize that it is all subject to change, it is of no permanence (see chapter 12, The Two Roads). And at the end of the day it is all without importance EXCEPT for the opportunities it has given us to develop the more positive sides of our being, such as 'love' in Rumi's language and not only his. (This word 'love' should also be the object of some deconstruction – see chapter 12.) What lasts is the good you do, the actions that are not prompted by personal gratification, or by responding to what Sri Aurobindo called our 'superficial faculty created by us in the course of our emergence from matter'. The Upanishad *Isha* deals with the question of life in the world – living our everyday lives – and life outside the world as an ascetic. This would seem especially relevant to what was said about Teresa and John of the Cross as regards their constant struggle to reform of the Carmelite Order. And the *Isha* Upanishad states that living only in the world leads to death and living only in the spirit leads to death also. But: 'They who devote themselves both to life in the world and to meditation, by life in the world overcome death, and by meditation achieve immortality.'

In a series of lectures given in Vienna by Rudolf Steiner in 1923 and focusing on the rebirth of the spiritual part of us, there is a page where he says that if we don't want 'to cross the threshold of death in a moribund daze but to cross the threshold of death with lucidity' then we must resurrect our souls using the divine forces within us. Where Golgotha and the death of Christ represent death followed by resurrection what we must aim for is resurrection (of our Self) and then death. In fact this question of being able to cross over from life to death with lucidity is a theme that Steiner returns to a number of times in different lectures. It is not unrelated to the Buddhist emphasis on the final thought-moment of the dying person or the way The Tibetan Book of the Dead aims at making the dying person conscious of what is to happen to him/her so that their attention is focused. In the Catholic Church also the prayers recited with a dying person seem to have the same purpose. It is sad to remark that for most of us in this modern world we live a life in which no thought or preparation at all is given to this important moment!

Sceptics over the ages have never ceased pointing out that any kind of immortality with our current body or even psyche does not make any kind of sense. And they have been perfectly right. Sceptics have long been aware of impermanence. And this focus on the transitory nature of things gives rise not unnaturally to the notion that if everything is called upon to disappear some day we should therefore enjoy things while we can. But if we follow what we have discussed above as regards the Self, there is a danger. The danger is that it may be taken to mean that we must forget or suppress or die to the personality that we have (or believe we have) in our everyday lives. In other words that we should not enjoy things. That has got to be a misunderstanding.

Death is an unattractive idea, certainly. And even more unattractive probably is the idea that in order to overcome death we must kill part of ourselves, the main part of our psyche. A premature death, it would seem. How many of us have balked in our youth at joining a religious movement because we felt it would mean we would have to relinquish our freedom? I did certainly. I think I felt that I would have to give up my independence, not be able to live my life, seek all kinds of experiences.

Yet religions have generally asked for obedience or submission. What do they offer in return?

Islam means 'submission', to God and to his Law. The reward is admission to Paradise.

Judaism has the Talmud which is the Law on how to live one's life. Following the Law creates a stable society blessed by God.

Christianity has (also) the Ten Commandments and the Sermon on the Mount of Jesus Christ, and the Catholic Church in particular has evolved a system of liturgy to be observed. The reward is resurrection on the Day of Judgement.

Hinduism states unequivocally that 'By devotion to Brahman and by indifference to the world does a man achieve immortality' (Upanishad Kaivalya). This leads to union with the Self and freedom from all attachments.

Buddhism has its eight precepts based on the awareness of old age, disease and death, the eight precepts being the beginning of the path towards *nirvana*, deliverance from the cycle of birth and rebirth.

Taoism teaches stripping away to reach the 'uncarved block'; being small, being unimportant will lead to the only Reality.

What is noticeable is that each religion demands some sacrifice and offers a reward in return. Apart from the fact that religions have sometimes and not rarely become instruments of political power, there is the simple question of the fairness of the deal. Is what we are being asked to give up worth the reward? Can we trust the offer? It is looking dangerously as if we may have to renounce our humanity, our personality, the ME we like (and sometimes hate). Or is it only the bad things about the Me that we would have to renounce? Sadly no. The higher Self, the permanent in us, is totally different from the self, the 'good' self that we know; it is separate from the mind, from the intellect, from the emotions; until we know it, it is unknown. A lot is being asked of us. Yet, to paraphrase what many mystics, spiritual teachers, saints and *gurus* have told us: *The less you see things as they really are, the less able you are to go through death.*

The mystics share a common denominator. And that is they behave as though the way to happiness and fulfilment is in being unselfish, seeing others as oneself, not giving in to self-gratification. But they do not say you should abandon the world. The Upanishad Isha expressly warns against that as something that would doom us to darkness. Work in the world is central.

In the Bhagavad-Gita Krishna says to Arjuna: 'Offer in thy heart all thy works to me, and see me as the end of thy love.' The importance then of working but not working for one's own benefit, though this need not mean we should not enjoy what we do.

When we try to live in that kind of way it is clear that we have constantly to exercise discrimination.

Another characteristic of the common denominator shared by the mystics is what they say about knowledge. It is certainly clear from Saint John of the Cross and Jalal-Ud-Din Rumi that knowledge of an intellectual kind does not have top priority. This brings in that other instrument of knowledge: intuition. Zen Buddhism has techniques to awaken intuition, and it is something we can also find in the work of Lao Zi which is the subject of the next chapter. It may be revealing to see how the Chinese, well-known for their pragmatism, approached the practical problem of dealing with the personality and our attachment to it.

Chapter 11

The Usefulness of What is Not

Strange ways of knowing

It is obvious that we are always reluctant to give up something that we see as useful and valuable to us. Or something to which we are attached and depend upon in our emotional life. Or something that quite simply gives us pleasure. More exactly, if we are to give up that thing, activity or person we need to become convinced that we are deluded in putting any value on it, or we need to find reasons to believe it is harmful. A friend who always believed in the usefulness of exercising one's right to vote in national and local elections, surprised me last year when he told me he had become disillusioned with our notion of democracy and had decided voting was a waste of time. I read of another person, an inveterate globetrotter, who has given up travelling by air because she feels strongly about the pollution caused by jet planes. I gave up eating meat years ago as I thought it wrong to kill animals and also not good for health. Yet I had enjoyed my meat and still think sometimes nostalgically of honey-cured ham or roast beef or that delicious Malaysian dish *beef rendang*. But something stronger than those partialities led me to give it up. Smoking is another example, and an interesting one. For here there is a question of addiction. The smoker can be aware and admit that smoking is not valuable to him and even ruinous financially. But it is still pleasurable and his body is powerfully addicted to it. When the smoker finally manages to give up cigarettes, he then realizes clearly that it was not valuable, useful, or even pleasurable. I read also of a famous singer, a millionaire, who decided to give up her singing career to devote herself to helping the poor in the most deprived areas of the world. She had given up something that was valuable to her. But for something that she thought to be more valuable. And I thought that was an important example. Value, after all, is a relative thing. There is no absolute value. Things are valuable only in relation to each other. I wondered how this reasoning applied to personality. We are attached to our personality; we don't like to think of giving it up. It's difficult to define it and difficult to describe how it is useful. But it is somehow valuable to us and we feel, I think, a certain pleasure in knowing that we are who we are – or who we think we are. For our own idea of ourselves may not be that of other people. So in this way we are attached to something much vaguer than cigarettes, travel, a career. But we are held to it by a feeling that if we do not attach importance to it we will have less pleasure in our life.

In a poem called 'What is this sacred dance?' Jalal-Ud-Din Rumi wrote:

> What is nobler than the soul? Yet when it leaves don't mourn:
> Something even more precious will take its place.

But what could take the place of our individual personalities?

I did not come across Taoism in any serious way until I lived in China. I had not realized that, while not derived itself from Buddhism, it had been a strong influence on Zen Buddhism and could account for a number of the particularities of Zen. 'Dao De Jing' is the book written by Lao Zi who lived in the sixth century before our era in China, though some think this Lao Zi may be a mythical character. It is the teaching in this book which is the foundation of Taoism, the traditional religion of China from that period up to the Communist revolution. But even now there are many Tao temples throughout the People's Republic and many practitioners. The Tao, along with Confucianism, underlies much Chinese thinking, as well as the Qigong, Tai Chi and the martial arts. Even in what we consider the materialistic, non-spiritual thinking of communist China, Lao Zi continues to have a pervading influence on the national way of thinking and it is to be found hidden behind many of the government policies and approaches in modern China.

There is a Tao temple near Xianning in Hubei Province on the borders with the neighbouring Hunan. It's a small monastery on a hillside stretching up from a very quiet valley. Low buildings, courtyards, silence. It was a spring day and sunny, the light played on the stone cobbles and the blue-tiled roofs. There were only a few monks and they were wrapped up in their occupations. Visitors didn't exist for them. A very pretty young woman minder guided me around. She was at least evidence that the state didn't forbid religion; though watching over it, not encouraging it. Worshippers were free to come as they pleased and I saw ten or fifteen, even a few young people. A middle-aged Chinese businessman from the nearby village came and told me how he had helped the temple with a considerable amount of money.

The Dao de Jing deals with three things: the universe, human life in the world and politics. There are certainly strange things in the Dao De Jing but some have a ring that is relevant to our modern age. Surely it cannot be that Lao Zi had ecology in mind when he wrote the following?

> Those that would gain what is under heaven by tampering with it – I have seen that they do not succeed.
>
> For that which is under heaven is like a holy vessel, dangerous to tamper with. Those that tamper with it, harm it.

It is certainly an exhortation to 'let it be'. And what about immigration?

> 'What large countries really need is more inhabitants; and what small countries need is some place where their inhabitants can go and get employment.' And how is this to be done?

> 'If a large kingdom can succeed in getting underneath a small kingdom then it will win the adherence of the small kingdom.' Colonialism, Imperialism, the European Union, the IMF and World Bank are all encapsulated in that!

Capital punishment?

> The people are not afraid of death; what then is the use of trying to intimidate them with the death penalty?
>
> There is the Lord of Slaughter always ready for this task, and to do it in his stead is like thrusting oneself into the master carpenter's place.

And society and the rule of law?

> The more prohibitions there are, the more ritual avoidances, the poorer people will be, The more laws are promulgated, the more thieves and bandits there will be.
>
> Therefore a sage has said: So long as I do nothing the people will of themselves be transformed.

And a lot of Dao De Jing is minimalist in that way.

'We put thirty spokes together and call it a wheel; but it is on the space where there is nothing that the usefulness of the wheel depends.'

True to this minimalist approach Lao Zi never mentions God. There is no personal God in Lao Zi. There is the 'always-so', the 'Great Concordance', the 'Self-so', states not beings.

Nor is death mentioned as such by Lao Zi. It is not a concern in itself. It is a non-subject.

'Tao is forever. He who possesses it, is not destroyed.'

To possess the Tao is to have the *power*. But paradoxically to have the power one must be weak like a child.

> The impunity of things fraught with the 'power'
> May be likened to that of an infant.
> Poisonous insects do not sting it, nor fierce beasts seize it,
> Nor clawing birds maul it.
> Its bones are soft, its sinews weak, but its grip is strong.
> Not yet to have known the union of male and female but to be completely formed,
> Means that the vital force is at its height;
> To be able to scream all day without getting hoarse
> Means that the harmony is at its perfection.
> To understand such harmony is to understand the always-so.

There are many of these paradoxes in Lao Zi. It is a view of life and living based on paradox and on opposites. Philosophy is often based on reason. So is Dao De Jing, but it is a different way of reasoning. Our usual logic would say that the weak depend on the strong, but Lao Zi asks:

> How did the great rivers and seas get their kingship over the hundred lesser streams?
>
> Through the merit of being lower than they.

And our common-sense logic tells that what is hard will overcome what is soft, or does it?

> Nothing under heaven is softer and more yielding than water; when it attacks things hard and resistant there is not one of them that can prevail.
>
> That the yielding conquers the resistant and the soft conquers the hard is a fact known by all men, yet utilized by none.

The core of Lao Zi is *quietness*. *Quietness* is non-action, detachment, being physically and emotionally uninvolved. But it is the 'Lord and Master' of activity. Activity, to have real value, must grow out of quietness. It is action without action: 'Tao never does; but through it all things are done.' Whether in the control of oneself or in the government of a kingdom quietness is the ability to know what is the minimum action needed and to do no more than that. Too much action will harm, says Lao Zi. Quietness is constantly remembering the end purpose that you wish and paring the means to suit that end purpose. Not doing anything unnecessary. And it is not giving prominence to the personality, to the ego. To be above the people, the sage, says the Tao, must speak as though he were lower than them. It is chipping away the useless accretions that have accumulated on ourselves and that hide the Uncarved Block which we should strive to get back to.

> In Tao the only motion is returning (to the Uncarved Block);
> The only useful quality, weakness.

'Strive' but not consciously for that would involve the ego. And it is not study and learning that can help us get back to the beginning for 'It was when intelligence and knowledge appeared, that the Great Artifice began'. And we must bear in mind that 'the greatest carver does the least cutting'. In order to guide his inner self or, in the case of a ruler, his subjects, the Sage can only be on top if he is under, and in this way he can achieve his aim: 'This he does by not striving; and because he does not strive, no one can contend with him'.

Returning to the state of the Uncarved Block, in quietness, the Sage comes to possess the Power, the power that is 'flimsy', inadequate, hidden and nameless yet supports all things.

One can see how language is forced to extremes to capture the meanings in the Tao. And language of course means names and that is when trouble starts for 'as soon as there are names, know that it is time to stop'. The Sage aims for the blankness of the unnamed for there lies the Power (which we can take as another word for Truth), and the 'inner light' which 'preserves us from all harm'.

Lao Zi relies greatly on taking language to the frontiers of nonsense to stimulate our awareness of his teaching.

> Though few know it, there is a bourn where there is neither right nor wrong;
> In a realm where every straight is doubled by a crooked, and every good by an ill,
> Surely mankind has gone long enough astray?
> Therefore the Sage
> Squares without cutting,
> Shapes the corners without lopping,
> Straightens without stretching,
> Gives forth light without shining.

Arthur Waley, one of the early translators of Lao Zi, tells us that the meaning of the last line is that the Sage reaches his ends without the use of means!

One of the most mysterious chapters in Lao Zi is chapter 6 which it is worth quoting in full:

> The Valley spirit never dies.
> It is named the Mysterious Female.
> And the doorway of the Mysterious Female
> Is the base from which Heaven and Earth sprang.
> It is there within us all the while;
> Draw upon it as you will, it never runs dry.

These lines cannot be understood by reason or logic. But approaching them with our intuition leads us to see the parallel with the Eternal Self, of the Hindu writings, or the 'Word' of Saint John ('*In the beginning was the Word...*'), the 'streams of living water' of Jalal-Ud-Din Rumi. Sri Aurobindo, in a commentary on the Upanishad Kena in which Uma speaks to Indra, says: 'Uma is the supreme source from which every action in the cosmos derives; it is from this supreme source and supreme consciousness that we should learn our own truth by reflecting it within ourselves.'

Lao Zi was conscious that not everyone agreed with what he said or understood him, which is not surprising for not only is what he says often obscure but many pieces that can be understood run counter to our usual practices and attitudes. 'My words are very easy to understand and to put into practice,' he says. 'Yet no one under Heaven understands them; no one puts them into practice.' He tells us that people say his teaching is madness, but it is just because it is great that it seems like folly, he retorts.

'As for things that do not seem like folly, well, there can be no question, about their smallness.'

Lao Zi deals with metaphysics and provides a methodology for living and in doing these explains the world we live in by two laws: antithesis and circular movement. Everything is set up in a system of opposites and makes sense because there are always opposites; it is essential to grasp both the positive and negative side of everything, understanding the negative side gives us a better understanding of the positive. And everything moves in a circular movement the end of which is a return to the beginning. The methodology is one of subtraction:

> Learning consists in adding to one's stock day by day;
> The practice of Tao consists of subtracting day by day,
> Subtracting and yet again subtracting
> Till one has reached inactivity.

It is clear that in the Tao the Self is distinct from body and mind, and that the sage should aim to divest himself/herself of material and personal interests and attachments. These characteristics are shared with Hinduism and Buddhism. 'Only he who rids himself forever of desire can see the secret essences,' Lao Zi announces in his very first chapter. In Lao Zi however there is no indication of where this message came from; there is no prophet (Lao Zi seems to have lived a totally retired life as a librarian), no revelation, no gods (as in Hinduism), no ritual or service of any kind, no mention of the sacrifices that pervade other beliefs; no heaven or hell. No punishment for wrong-doing. It is a truly minimalist religion.

But religion remains the right word. What is the aim?

1. Tao is how to be fulfilled in your life. And fulfilment in life means knowledge of the 'secret essences', the 'Mysterious Female', the 'uncarved block'.
2. And this is achieved by simplifying and subtracting; by finding balance/harmony without complication.

There are similarities with Hinduism and both the Upanishads and the Bhagavad-Gita existed before Lao Zi. There must have been a lot of contact, commercial and other, between India and China in those times. But even so Lao Zi seems remarkably independent and seems to stand alone in the midst of his own vision. It would be even more difficult, on account of dates, to propose any link to Buddhism which is believed to have arrived in China in the first century of our era. Despite the fact that the Buddha lived in the period 585 to 500 BC and Lao Zi 623–543, so another 43 years after Lao Zi's death, it seems unlikely that the teaching of the Buddha had any influence on the Tao. There are however interesting parallels, for example in the question of the importance of discrimination. Several times in Lao Zi we are told that the Sage 'takes this but rejects that'. In the Bardo Thötröl (The Tibetan Book of the Dead) the ability to discriminate is the antidote to desire, passion and grasping at things and is linked to the *Tathagata Amitabha* (see chapter 2, page 19). References to the Void in Lao Zi make one think of the limitless, all-pervading space of the *Dharmadhatu*. But The Tibetan Book of the Dead, at least in the form we know it, is later than Lao Zi so in which direction was there influence if any? It is clear, I think, that Lao Zi is a particularly original statement of the eternal truths that are to be found in the ancient Hindu texts and in esoteric Buddhism though there is no indication of direct influences. In comparison, while it is easy to find influences of the Old Testament and of Christianity in Islam, and the influence of Judaism in Christianity, the Tao has stood very much by itself. Perhaps it would be better to look in ancient China itself for influences. And maybe they are to be found in the *Book of Change,* a very old and mysterious collection of barely comprehensible texts.

The Book of Change is the earliest work of Chinese philosophy. It is anonymous and the exact date of its composition is not known but it can be assumed to date from maybe more than the second millennium BC. The Book of Change uses the symbol of the hexagram to express the constant changes in life. The hexagram is made up of continuous lines (representing yang or positive force) or broken lines (representing yin, or negative force) and the number and position of the unbroken lines tells you about the position of the qi or vital energy (either in the world or the individual or indeed in anything). Thus:

— —
— —
— —
— —
— —
— —

means all yin or in other words that the yang qi is at its lowest, the vital energy has gone deep inside you, or deep into the earth as in winter. The next step is:

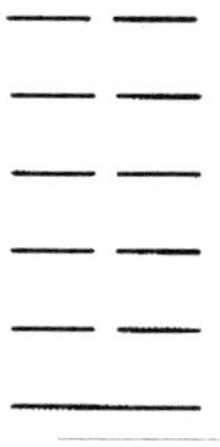

when the yang qi begins to grow or to move towards exteriorization. In terms of an annual calendar the first of these two diagrams corresponds to a period towards the end of the year – October – and the second, when qi begins to rise, corresponds to the next period or November, reckoned a good time to practise qigong. And when we observe nature attentively we can see that the first buds appear not after the winter solstice as we might have thought but in November. So the sequence goes on until you get all yang with six unbroken lines.

Above all the Book of Change represents the different cycles in our lives, and the fact that everything is cyclic. Our lives, our careers, our marriages, our children, and nature itself, day and night, seasons, the evolution of the earth. The Book of Change also tells of the Spirit which supports everything, which is the giver and sustainer of all physical life, which is fundamentally cyclic: winter, summer; rise, fall; health, illness; life, death. In this way the Book of Change reminds us of the smallness of our place in creation. It tells us there is a Law that is much greater than us. As the Bhagavad-Gita put it: 'Thus was the Wheel of the Law set in motion and that man lives indeed in vain who in a sinful life of pleasures helps not in its revolutions.' And also: 'All actions take place in time by the interweaving of the forces of nature; but the man lost in selfish delusion thinks he himself is the actor.'

This philosophy, embodied in the Book of Change, which is all about cycles and rhythms, led to the development of gymnastic exercises designed to regulate the correct flow of *qi* in the body for upon this correct flow of qi depends the full enjoyment of life and the preservation of health. Illness therefore arises from an internal disharmony and not from an external aggression which is the basis of most of modern western medicine. It is said that the gymnastic movements were choreographed by Taoist monks who observed the movements of certain animals such as the crane, the tortoise, the snake and the deer, seeing these movements as corresponding to natural energy flows. In executing their movements the monks began to observe that energy flowed along certain paths in their bodies which they could feel. These paths became the meridians of traditional Chinese medicine.

Tao has something of the characteristics of mystics like the Sufis, or like William Law[1] whom Huxley describes as having been 'for all his talents, absurdly simple and single-minded'. Law can never have heard of the Tao which first appeared in translation in Europe (in French) in 1842. But there is a ring of Lao Zi in much of his writing such as:

> There is a root or centre of thee from which all these faculties come forth, as lines from a centre, or as branches from the body of a tree. This depth is called the centre, the fund or the bottom of the soul. This depth is the unity, the eternity – I had almost said the infinity of thy soul; for it is so infinite that nothing can satisfy it or give it rest but the infinity of God.
> (William Law, quoted in The Perennial Philosophy, Aldous Huxley)

However there is an eminently practical, pragmatic side to Lao Zi which is absent in most of the mystics for it deals at the same time with human life and with politics. In Tao the mastery of the self is equivalent and parallel to the mastery of a nation; the government of oneself and of a nation follow the same methodology.

> Ruling a large kingdom is like cooking a small fish. They who

> by Tao ruled all that is under heaven, did not let an evil spirit within them display its powers. Nay, it was not only that the evil spirit did not display its powers; neither was the Sage's good spirit used to the hurt of other men. Nor was it only that his good spirit was not used to hurt other men, the Sage himself was thus saved from harm. And so each being saved from harm, their powers could converge towards a common end.

The Tao in other words is more WHOLE, and for all its opacity, more practical and there lies is its strength. Like the message it conveys the strength of the Tao is a hidden strength, a seeming weakness even.

The Tao says we should go on subtracting and subtracting, until the ego and its selfishness disappear along with purely material desires. It doesn't provide DOs and DON'Ts of an ethical kind. If you manage to reach the condition of the 'uncarved block' you will automatically behave correctly. And – and this is important – you will be able to live in the practical world. That point is of great importance for too often we have been told that we should forsake the world, give it up entirely.

It is very clear, I thought, from the writings of Lao Zi that not only well-being but also, according to him, success in the world, depended on diminishing the place of the personality, the ego. 'Subtracting', becoming small, 'weaker', chipping away at the accretions of the ego are constant themes. And they are also for Hinduism and Buddhism. We have seen (chapter 9) the way Buddhism views the notion of personality as a fiction. In Hinduism the Bhagavad-Gita, like the Tao, is anchored in action in the world but in action that is not done for oneself or for selfish reasons. Krishna says to Arjuna: 'Whatever you do, or eat, or give, or offer in adoration, let it be an offering to me.' And in another place he says: 'Consecrate all thy work to me; by mere doing actions in my service thou shalt attain perfection.' And also: 'And these (who consecrate their works to me) I very soon deliver from the ocean of death and life-in-death.' 'Perfection' can mean indestructibility, beyond further change. In the 'ocean of death', we drown, and in our lives, without the 'secret essences', the 'Power', the 'inner light' we live a life-in-death. So this yielding of the ego is not without its reward. Lao Zi talks of the 'secret essences' which come from the practice of the Tao and the renunciation of desires. So it looks as if this renunciation of self leads to something more valuable.

The Tao is not based on what we know as logic or reason. There is another kind of understanding at work. Lao Zi uses a variety of words to talk about the underlying reality. He calls it 'the Power', the 'secret essences', the 'uncarved block', the 'always-so', the 'Mysterious Female' and more. This refusal to use a single term is important. A single term limits the meaning, brings in definition and logic; the multiple terms open the way to intuition. In the same way, I think, that in some beliefs there are many names for God. One could argue, paradoxically, that a single name for God leads to idolatry!

Lao Zi is talking of something eternal within us, something that is not subject to death, though he never puts it bluntly in those terms. It is as if he is talking about the visible and the invisible and saying that what is valuable is the invisible, and that it is precisely the invisible that is permanent. It is exactly as it was in chapter 4 (p. 44), where permanence and eternity were to be found beyond the *sephirot* in the realm of what seems like nothingness.

It remained to be seen what this meant in the face of our everyday lives and the demands and problems we have to confront daily. That is the subject of the following chapter.

Throughout all of this rings a message, sometimes softly, sometimes more emphatically. It is we should not renounce the world and our enjoyment of it and that in fact a fundamental message of all our major traditions has been not only to prepare for the transformation of death but to live fully our life on earth. And indeed that is only common sense. If we have the benefit of this life on earth in the physical world it is evident that it must have some purpose or other. If a lot of the things we do in our lives are in the long term a waste of time and futile then surely there must be some other purpose or content to this life of ours. The challenge is in finding that purpose and discovering how best one should live this life – in terms of its usefulness of course and in terms of our own sense of fulfilment. But at the same time to understand the nature of death and how it links with life.

Part Three

The Harmony of Life and Death

Chapter 12

The Two Roads

Overcoming death by life in the world

It is around us all the time. At every instant death is around us though we don't pay attention. It is in the changing seasons, in the air we breathe which loses its life before we exhale it. In the plants we eat, or the animals. The cells of our body are constantly dying and renewing themselves. Death, like life, is one of the aspects of matter, and we can say no more than that. And when we look at matter we see that everything renews itself, nothing dies. So perhaps we should not see death and life as being in opposition to each other.

The aim of this book is to explore the nature of death, and how different traditions, religions and cultures can help us understand it and deal with it. And especially to try to see if, as some cultures teach, it is complementary to life, another way of living. For obviously it has to be a different way of living, without the physical body we know. If this is so, then how does a person get prepared for this event, for surely some familiarization would be useful if not necessary? The issue of renouncing the self, or subordinating our ego to some other (greater?) cause, has been a constant in what the different formal religions tell us, in one way or another. That much is clear, even if it is not always totally clear what this might entail. For what exactly does this renunciation of self mean and what are the implications, for each of us, for the way we live our lives in the world we know? The key seems to be there, in how we are to understand personality and our place in the world of action. The problem of the detail remains.

The two roads are the road of the world and the road of withdrawal from the world into the spirit. Talking of our place in the world a related issue, and an important one, is the place of 'I' and the place of 'we'. Our focus cannot be just the 'I'. We are all part of a society, part of a whole. Whatever experiences we have are often things we have to go through alone but our lives are unavoidably bound up with other people. And according to a number of our world religions the nature of our behaviour towards other people will determine our afterlife. It is as if other people were put there to test us. To test us as personalities, or, perhaps, to use the language of the Vedanta, to allow us to find our Self. In the Gnostic Gospel of Saint Thomas we find Jesus saying: 'Perhaps people think that I have come to cast peace upon the world. They do not know that I have come to cast conflicts upon the earth: fire, sword, war. For there will be five in a house: there'll be three against two and two against three, father against son and son against father, and they will stand alone.' Relationships may not be all sweetness and light but perhaps those conflicts are what is necessary for the development of our Self. At the end of the day we stand alone with the responsibilities that result from our relationships.

At a lunch party not so long ago in Bamako, Mali, there were several nuns, my wife and myself and our hostess. Our hostess declared that the most important thing was for us all to love one another. One of the nuns sighed. Perhaps she felt that it's all very well to say these things but she had been trying for years and... One could go further, and say that we shouldn't say such things at all. We don't know what love is. There can hardly be a word in our languages that is more overused and more in need of deconstruction than the word 'love'. Consider the meaning of love in the following:

1. But true love is a durable fire,
In the mind ever burning,
Never, sick, never dead, never cold,
From itself never turning.

(From: 'The Holy Land of Walsinghame')
2. He loves football.
3. With best wishes, love, David
4. My little, children, let us not love in word, neither in tongue; but in deed and in truth.
5. Those who believe love Allah more than (anything else).

But there is not only love, there is also hate. Love and hate, attraction and aversion, two not opposing but complementary forces. We human beings live a lot in the world of our emotions. And these emotions are dominated by the twin forces of attraction and repulsion. In fact, as Heindel, the Rosicrucian mystic and writer, and others have pointed out, we need both these forces in our make-up. We are attracted to certain things and we repel others. In the normal and desirable course of events we are attracted to things that are good for us, and our fellow human beings, and reject those things that are not. Heindel says that the force of repulsion operates MAINLY in the lower part of our universe of emotions, where those emotions are the most negative and the most destructive. In this way the force of repulsion is our friend and not our enemy.

One cannot help being reminded of the forces described in quantum physics. The strong force and the weak force. The strong force is what allows particles to hold together. The electro-magnetic force cannot explain how several protons (which are positively charged) can exist together in a nucleus without being forced apart. The strong force holds them together. The weak force is connected to 'beta decay' where a neutron isolated from the nucleus will decay into an electron and a proton within a few minutes, but the resulting mass is much less than the original neutron. To physicists this 'decay' was evidence of the existence not only of another particle but of another force. And this other particle must have zero mass or it would have been observed. This new particle came to be known as the neutrino and is in fact an 'anti-particle' and became critical in nuclear physics.

Love is the element that can bind humans. You can't SEE love. Sometimes you can't see the effects of love. The real strong force in quantum physics is the 'gluons' which glue quarks together. It is extremely powerful but not evident to us in our everyday lives. Significantly perhaps, it operates over very short distances. The weak force in quantum physics could be seen as negative, it destroys, it subtracts. It is potentially destructive as in nuclear fusion, and it is linked to separation and not union. Does it operate over greater distances? One thing is certain, sadly, and that is that it is easier to hate than to love. It is easier to understand what hatred is than it is to understand what love is. It's worth noting also that while there is no known limit to high temperatures there is a limit to how low the thermometer can go (around -273°C). Love is positive and involves adding; hatred is negative and means subtracting. But as Lao Zi maintained it is important that we continue subtracting and subtracting until we reach the 'uncarved block'. So that subtracting force is also necessary. Love leads to attachments, additions, which can be burdens on the Self. Those burdens need to be lightened and so subtraction comes in. The question is what is subtracted from what? Do we subtract only the bad? Is that possible and do we have that kind of choice? We are tottering on the edge of a sort of mystery here, not far from madness. Without hatred there would have been no Crucifixion. For Christians, if there had been no Crucifixion… But then, if love had been the only principle there would have been no need for Crucifixion.

I remembered something that had once puzzled me. It was told to me by a friend who was a disciple of a spiritual Master or guru with a large and devoted following. During an address to his followers the Master had one day said things to them (some of them had been his disciples for over 30 years) that aroused their anger and incomprehension, and set many against him. As if he was trying to make them hate him. But he was playing perhaps with the twin forces of attraction and repulsion. He was, it seemed to me now, trying to cut them free from him, because their emotional attachment to him was a burden to them. It was preventing them from reaching their true Selves. That, reaching their true Selves, was to him more important that the emotional ties they had to him. They needed to build their boats and their boats did not need to be overloaded. They needed to trim their sails... Gilgamesh used one pole at a time and each one only once. No attachment, no dependence.

We must note that the number 2 leads to multiplicity. It is the opposite of Unity, of Oneness. So 2 means trouble. Love between human beings is often about two people and often leads to trouble – and when it gets to three there is even more trouble... In theory then the best and most favourable environment for love would be 1. Subtraction at work! This is a point worth looking at. Nietzsche, always controversial, said: 'You pay a lot of attention to your neighbour and your attention expresses itself in fine words. But I say to you: your love of your neighbour is no more than your imperfect love of yourself'. And later in the same chapter: 'I would like neighbours to become unbearable for you; you would then be forced to draw from within yourself the friend who has a heart brimming with love.' He maintained that we preach love for our neighbour as a means of escaping from ourselves: what is not ourselves is seen as better than ourselves. But it is within ourselves that we have to find love.

And this 'love', what is it exactly? Complicated... that is the problem, and was probably Nietzsche's problem for he saw hypocrisy and falseness, at worst, and ignorance at best, in what we call 'love of our neighbour'.

This neighbourly love that Nietzsche attacks is in a way bound up with the intellect and with what the intellect tells us we *should* do. Saint Paul in his well-known passage on love, or 'charity' (*caritas*), made several key points. Love is not the intellect, it is not knowledge. It is not faith either, and it is not generosity; you can give away all your possessions, even sacrifice your body, 'if I have no love, this does me no good'. One is beginning to ask oneself what this mysterious 'love' or 'charity' may be. Then Paul tells us 'love is eternal' (the older version of the Bible in English says 'charity faileth not'). So love then is something distinct from us, from our bodies or our minds and our emotions even, for none of those is eternal, and they can each fail. Love is something greater than us. Is it the friend inside with the 'heart brimming with love' that Nietzsche talked about? And is that not the Self?

So it is not love alone that makes the world go round, it is the forces of attraction and repulsion: the two forces that hold the universe together. We find these also in *The Tibetan Book of the Dead*. Akshobhya, the deity of the second day after death, represents hatred and aggression, forces of repulsion. Amitabha, the deity of the fourth day, represents passion and desire. Both contain their opposites, Akshobhya contains the possibility of critical analysis, and Amitabha contains discrimination so that passion can convert to compassion.

Just as love and hatred are not opposing forces but complementary forces so life in the world and the spiritual life need not be seen as exclusive. The Upanishad *Isha* has already been quoted (see chapter 10, page 100) as saying that a life of meditation alone is not enough. Very significantly a few verses after that we read that: 'To darkness are they doomed who worship only the body, and to greater darkness they who worship only the spirit.' The Koran points to the things men covet but without condemning them, only to say that Allah has other, better things. Nowadays we regularly meet people who intuitively feel a need for spirituality but are hesitant because it seems to mean giving up what they enjoy. But living with the things we covet, living with passion and desire are part of the road. Our path through life is to be seen as a movement between external activity and a growth of inner spirituality. The return to religion we can sometimes observe in people when they grow old is not just a piece of opportunism. There may be cases where the movement towards inner spirituality is faster than in others. Gautama Buddha was born into a royal family, enjoyed luxury and married the beautiful Yasodhara, living in a world of palaces, servants and fine food, until he abandoned all of that for a contemplative life. In oriental thinking, however, this movement can span incarnations. Indeed, the Buddha himself must have had other incarnations in which his focus was mainly on life in the world. In all cases, at least if we follow the usual Hindu or Buddhist teaching, it will be a question of a number of incarnations to reach a deep sense of spirituality. And so all that time spent in 'things of the world' must be for a purpose. For the words in the *Isha* have an important implication. Which is that life in the world is necessary, in the sense that we can only learn in the world not in meditation or in life in the spirit. Rudolf Steiner draws attention to this also when he says that after death we cannot develop, we can develop only through experiences in the physical world. This can cause us much pain after death for we would often like to have new contexts to experiment lessons we have learnt and we come to yearn for another physical life so as to do this. One contemporary spiritual leader with a large following in Asia and disciples in many western countries, said once, 'It is only in this physical form that we can rise above the three worlds and free ourselves from the cycle of life and death.' So no one should dream of taking away from youth the desire for action, the joys and anguish of passion, the thrill of being really alive. Nor can we take away the will to fight injustices, to take sides for what we believe is right, to combat poverty, illness, war. The reluctance of a number of people to take a more spiritual path in life is not only due to their reluctance to give up the things they enjoy but also the fear of giving up their personality. But the personality, as it was analyzed in the preceding chapters, is something that is vague and fragile. It is tied up with the traditions and beliefs of the society we have grown up in – would our personality be the same if we were born in a different culture? It is also bound up with the events that have marked our lives and often with what seem like trivial events – the words of parents or friends, relatives or teachers, that have somehow stuck in our minds and guide our beliefs and actions. It is, however, a road we have to go along, on the way to realizing its insignificance in any permanent sense. Gradually an awareness of the smallness of the self grows, and a parallel awareness of the key things that emerge from this, which are:

1. We need to become able to dissociate ourselves from the past, from an obsession with it, while being able to step back and see it objectively (our past actions) as what has formed the present.
2. We need to focus on that present which will in its turn create the future and concentrate on BEING rather than on DOING, what we ARE rather than what we do. What we do will follow from what we are.

Following these two guidelines can make us masters of ourselves. Ruminating *obsessively and unproductively* about the past and dreaming of the future are things we do constantly, as part of the human condition, but in that way we live an unreal life. The only thing that is real is the present moment, however fleeting it may be. But that present moment has been created by the past and will create the future.

This issue of life in the world and withdrawal from the world has also been a central preoccupation of Christianity. Liberation theology on the one hand, retreat into a Trappist monastery on the other. The case of Mary and Martha in the Bible is generally interpreted as the contrast between the person who is busy with worldly affairs and the contemplative. There are three places where we can come across these two sisters in the New

Testament. The first one is related by Luke and in this scene Jesus visited the two sisters who lived in Bethany, a few miles from Jerusalem. While Jesus was in their house Martha busied herself with housework and could not find time to attend to him. Mary, on the other hand, sat at Jesus' feet and listened to his teaching. Eventually Martha complained to Jesus about her sister and suggested he should tell her to help with the work. Jesus told her she (Martha) was too worried and troubled by many things when 'just one is needed'. He went on to say that Mary had chosen 'that good part' (the 'just one' that is necessary) and it would 'not be taken away from her'. In other words she had successfully subtracted the superfluous in her life. So it seems that Mary wins the approval ratings at this point and that contemplation wins over action in the world. But maybe it is not so clear-cut. The second meeting with the two sisters, related by John, is after the death of Lazarus, their brother. Jesus decided to go to Bethany. Before he arrived in the village Martha, who must have abandoned whatever duties bound her to her home when she heard of his being near, came and met him on the road whereas Mary stayed in the house. Martha showed unmistakable faith in Jesus saying she believed he could resurrect her brother. Martha fetched Mary to greet Jesus. Curiously Mary did not show the same immediate faith in Jesus' power but wept at the loss of her brother. She was engrossed in her grief in the same way that her sister on the first visit was engrossed in her duties. It is almost as if they had changed roles. What to make of it? This is not a parable of course, it is an account of an event in the life of Jesus. But like many other accounts of events in the life of Jesus, quite apart from whatever literal meaning they may have, the spiritual meaning of it needs to be pierced. I find that the most accessible spiritual meaning is that Mary and Martha are both present in all of us. Sometimes we are busy in the world and sometimes we are introverted and wish to connect to the spirit. Faith can be strong even in the person who works in the world, and can be weak in the person drawn to contemplation and meditation or prayer. But, and it is an important 'but', there is only one thing that is necessary and that is the connection to the spirit. And the hustle and bustle of life can distract us from that connection as we can be 'worried and troubled' as Martha was on the first visit of Jesus. And that connection to the spirit, says Jesus, shall not be taken away. Just as the Bhagavad-Gita says in the words of Krishna: 'When he sees me in all and all in me, then I never leave him and he never leaves me.'

The story of Mary and Martha runs parallel to the story of the raising of Lazarus from death. The theme of death and overcoming death is dominant in all these verses about the family of Mary and Martha: the death of Lazarus and the impending death of Jesus who took a great risk in coming back to Bethany where he narrowly escaped death by stoning not long before. We know that Jesus will overcome death in his resurrection but what of Lazarus? How are we to interpret his return to life, when Jesus for the first time brought back to life a person who had been dead for four days? First of all it is clear from the text that Jesus was close to this family of Lazarus and his two sisters. But when the news of Lazarus' death reached him he did not go immediately. He waited for two days which meant that when he eventually got back to Bethany Lazarus had been dead for four days. This is usually taken to mean that he was to attempt the impossible. The contemporary Jewish belief was that the soul stayed close to the body for three days and after that left it finally and completely. We then have one of the most dramatic scenes in the New Testament. Jesus is taken to the tomb of Lazarus. He insists that the stone covering the entrance be removed despite Martha's warning that there will be a 'stinking smell' for Lazarus has been dead for four days. The stone is removed. Jesus prays to God and orders Lazarus to come out. Before a number of witnesses frozen with suspense, not knowing what to expect, Lazarus, wrapped in his funeral cloths, comes out, somewhat unsteadily one imagines... Some of the witnesses, we are told, became converted to Jesus on seeing this miracle but some went to the Pharisees and reported the event. That was when the decision to kill Jesus was taken by the Chief Priest. So the Lazarus event is a critical event on the path to the crucifixion. But how exactly are we to interpret it? That Lazarus died of an illness and was brought back to life after four days? But what would be the point? To prove Jesus' ability to work miracles and at the same time prepare his later fate? Maybe. A more spiritual interpretation is also possible. Rudolf Steiner says that we are looking at an account of an initiation. The ancient mysteries of Egypt and Greece demanded that the initiate be put in a state as close to death as possible for several days before being 'resurrected' as an enlightened person. Hence the fact that Jesus waited for two more days and did not seem unduly worried about Lazarus. And when he was moved and wept it was because of the suffering of the family and villagers not over Lazarus. If this was an initiatic event the Lazarus who came out of the tomb (and is the tomb not a piece of symbolism in the re-telling?) was not the Lazarus who entered it. He emerged with a developed spiritual body. He was the first Christian initiate. The tomb and the noisome smell would then represent the physical body and the old self associated with it. Lazarus was a new man. He had now built his boat and could cross from life to death with full consciousness. We hear of him once more in the Gospel of John. Six days before the Passover Jesus returned to Bethany, to the home of Lazarus and his sisters. There was a dinner for him. 'Lazarus was one of those sitting at the table with Jesus.' It hardly seems necessary to mention this but it is mentioned and it is the last mention of Lazarus. What are we to make of it? There is a mystery in the presence of Lazarus at that dinner in Bethany. He says nothing and nothing more is said about him except that the authorities would like to have him killed because 'on his account many were rejecting them and believing in Jesus'. Just because he was brought back from the dead? Or because it was evident that he had become enlightened and was living proof not that Jesus could resurrect the dead but that he could impart the spirit of God to others, bring enlightenment to them? What is important for the content of this chapter is that the presence of Lazarus at that dinner, the mere mention of his PRESENCE, says that he was still active in the world, even though he had been initiated into the mysteries of life and death, into the world of the spirit. It is confirming that a spiritual life must be complemented by a role in the world. In this way the role of Lazarus fits in perfectly harmoniously with the story of the two sisters, Martha and Mary.

The whole story concerning Mary, Martha and Lazarus is covered with a veil of mystery. It does, however, point to the two roads and the two worlds: the world of the spirit and the physical world. Martha and Mary represent the two worlds separately, in Lazarus they are combined, there is the body, the tomb, and the body after enlightenment. The body after enlightenment, the new Lazarus, is present at a dinner and the authorities think he is influential enough to be a danger. He has abandoned the old self but he continues to live in the world. And to face danger and death. But that cannot perturb him for, as a result of his initiation, he had the 'one thing that is needed and which cannot be taken away from him'.

The theme of action in the world and withdrawal from the world is central to the Bhagavad-Gita. This philosophical song of eighteen chapters is set in a much, much longer epic poem, the *Mahabharata* which tells the story of the war between good and evil represented by the two great families, the Pandavas and Kuravas. During a pause in the fighting, Arjuna, a prince of the Pandavas, talks to his charioteer. He is deeply upset because he sees himself aligned in battle against people he knows, people who are relatives even, and whom he has loved. He recoils at the thought that he may have to kill them. The charioteer turns out to be the God Krishna and Krishna explains many things to

Arjuna over the eighteen chapters, among them the fact that he must do the duty that has fallen to him and so fulfil his destiny. Krishna points out that Arjuna is wrong to regret the death of his enemies even if they are former friends and relatives. Nothing dies: 'The wise grieve not for those who live; and they grieve not for those who die – for life and death shall pass away.' Arjuna shouldn't be troubled by something that is eternal and cannot die, cannot be killed – the eternal spirit in man. Arjuna, says Krishna, should simply carry on doing the work he has been given to do. But apart from the fact that death is an illusion there is another reason why Arjuna must continue his fight. That reason is that it is his duty, his *karma*, in this life. If he tries to avoid this fight it would be 'fall into transgression'. No matter what the outcome. Arjuna must accept victory or defeat with the same peace in his soul. The important thing is not to want an outcome for his personal pleasure. Work that is done for a personal reward has no value in terms of 'the Yoga of wisdom'. The Gita moves on from the external battle that is Arjuna's immediate preoccupation to the inner struggle of man to find his spirit, his Self. And the same rules of battle apply, says Krishna. It is through actions in the world that he will find his Self. Every man has his work to do in life and no one can renounce that, but the sage must renounce the reward for his work. So the key thing is to renounce reward, personal reward. You work for others or for God, if you have identified one. In fact, a little reflection would persuade us that it is not at all necessary to work consciously for God or a God, what is important is the unselfish nature of the work. We should remember, I think, that in the Hindu system the God within us, the Self, is the same as the God without. Whatever is done must be done as an offering to the Self, not to the lower self:

> Whatever you do, or eat, or give, or offer in adoration, let it be an offering to me; and whatever you suffer, suffer it for me.

> Thus thou shalt be free from the bonds of karma, which yield fruits that are evil and good; and with thy soul one in renunciation thou shalt be free and come to me.
>
> (Bhagavad-Gita 9)

Doing everything for Krishna and offering everything to Krishna, is merely another way of saying, 'Act selflessly.' The resolution of the conflict between action in the world and the spiritual life lies, as the *Isha* Upanishad said, in the fact that both are necessary. But one can only keep alive the Self, which is important for the passage into death, if one performs actions for something other than the satisfaction of the personal self. So there is no question of turning one's back on the need to engage in action of all kinds; such an engagement can even be the duty of certain among us. In our western culture the topic of 'ethics' was at best a lukewarm topic for those born in the middle of the 20th century. The effects of the world financial crisis with its associated scandals, the low-intensity wars, the increase in the number of starving in the world and the flow of illegal immigrants towards the developed countries may have changed that attitude. One thing is sure: when it comes to the subject of life and death ethics is central. At the heart of unethical behaviour lies egoism. So action alone, however magnificent, however impressive, is not enough. Gilgamesh's quest for immortality failed because he was too much bound up with himself, with his own glory and his own renown which he wanted to be everlasting.

The Cabbala seems a strange place to look for answers to this apparent conflict between action and contemplation. But the *sephirot* are a vivid representation of the how the world of the spirit relates to the material world. Looking at the diagram below one can see that the most spiritual *sephirot* at the very top belong to the world of emanations. This is the domain of *Kether,* God, of *Hokmah,* the Word, and of *Binah,* divine intelligence. The next level is the world of creation. But creation here means conception, plan. We are not in the world of physical matter yet.

The next level is the world of formation. In this world we find *Netzach*, the domain of the *Elohim*, who, the Bible says, created the world. And of Hod, the kingdom of Raphael and the sciences that rule our lives. And of the Moon, in the *sephira Yesod*, ruling the rhythms of our material and psychic lives. And only then do we get to *Malkhuth*, the world of action, the material world in which we live. It is the world we live in, the world we are MEANT and DESTINED to live in, but it is nevertheless permeated by the presence of all the other levels right up to *Kether*. And we are not meant to cut ourselves off from those levels, we are meant to allow them to come into our material world of action, *Malkhuth*, to be reflected in it. They are the 'one thing needed', our connection to the spiritual world.

Kether

(The world of emanations)

Binah **Hokmah**

Geburah **Heshed**

(The world of creation)

Tiphereth

Hod **Netzach**

(The world of formation)

Yesod

Malkhuth -the earth ***(The world of action)***

Figure 3: The different worlds

The term 'spiritual world' has been used in the above account. There is always a danger and a weakness in the terms we use. They connect us to aspects of our cultures and belief systems; the term 'field' could have been used to describe the non-physical world. When we talk of 'mind' we mean more than our mind, more than the one we associate with our brain. As time passes in this 21st century we find more and more evidence of things like telepathy, and other cases of transfer of information that cannot be explained in purely physical terms. They are part of mind in its wider meaning, as something bigger than us and which governs matter, if you like. Deepak Chopra in his book, *Life After Death,* gives a number of examples. Everything cannot be explained as having a physical basis. Is the brain the creator of the mind, or the mind the creator of the brain? Deepak Chopra gives a number of reasons and examples of experiments that support the second alternative. The brain is like a radio that receives signals from outside it. 'That which is not comprehended by the mind, but by which the mind comprehends, know that to be Brahman', says the Upanishad *Kena*.

We are mind and matter; but we are in a position to understand the nature of matter much more easily than the nature of mind. So as long as we are in a physical body matter tends to predominate. We are therefore often at the mercy of opposite forces, of attraction and repulsion, of love and hate, of peace and war... And, necessarily, of good and evil. We see a lot of things around us that we can qualify as 'evil'. Since we must live in the world of *Malkhuth* and act in the world of *Malkhuth,* is it not worth looking more closely at the place and role of what we may call 'evil'?

Chapter 13

It's Not All Black and White

The old problem of good and evil

Is what we term 'evil' ignorance of one's true Self and behaving in a way that doesn't take account of the harmony of life and death? What was termed the true Self in earlier chapters would transcend life and death and create a harmony between them. Anything attached to the ego only, to purely selfish ends, would exist only in life, and end with death. Gilgamesh was our example. But is it as simple as that? That is a question which this chapter and the next one after it try to answer.

As children we see religion as something that teaches us to be good and behave well. What is the point of being good? A question many people at one time or another, even believers, ask themselves. The reward, if any, is uncertain and distant and if there is a price to pay for not being good, may it not be worth it? And in a world where we see daily suffering of millions on our television screens, we may ask ourselves indeed if God exists and if he does, is he himself good to allow so much suffering?

This behaviour of ours, be it good or bad, what effect does it have on our death and whatever comes after? Christianity and Islam have similar and clear messages: the nature of your afterlife, heaven or hell, depends on the quality of your behaviour in this life. The Torah does not explicitly talk of an afterlife, it wants us to focus on this life, but the existence of heaven and hell are clear from many references. The Jewish belief is that when a person dies and goes to heaven, the soul is given two films to watch. One relates the actual events of the person's life objectively and the other shows what would have been the case if the person had behaved better. It is an occasion for regret and often for anguish. So for Jews heaven and hell exist and are eternal just as they are in the other two monotheistic faiths.

The oriental religions, Hinduism and Buddhism, base their morality on the two concepts of reincarnation and *karma*. It is probably not useful to talk of 'good' or 'bad' actions for good and bad are relative in the end. But it IS the case that all actions produce *karma*, which may positively or negatively impact on the person later in his or her present life or in a future life. The Upanishad *Brihadaranyaka* draws attention to the limited effects of doing good: 'Even if a man, ignorant of the Self, should do virtuous deeds on earth, he would not arrive through them at everlasting life; for the effects of his deeds would be finally exhausted.' The person would derive some benefits from having done good but those benefits would not be lasting and would not be enough to lead to freedom from the trials of physical reincarnation. Something else is necessary. Is it the 'just one that is needed' that Jesus talked of to Martha, the constant connection to the spirit? The Tao, for its part, avoids establishing criteria for what is good or bad. The only aim is to reach the ultimate simplicity of one's being and in doing so, concepts like good and bad fade into insignificance and lose their usefulness.

Traditionally evil is associated with the Devil. The Devil and demons are the 'declared enemies' of man, says the Koran, they see us even if we cannot see them. We must not listen to them. But they fear God who was their creator. In this way, and it is mentioned in the Old Testament also, the powers of evil are servants of God, are part of a Grand Design. We need somehow or other to be clearer about what the major religions have to say about this Grand Design and the place in it of Good and Evil. For this issue of good and evil seems to be inseparable from any harmony that there may be between life and death.

We have all the same kind of yardsticks for Good and Evil. Mother Teresa, Al-Hallaj, Abraham are good, Adolph Hitler, the butchers of Srebrenica and Caligula are bad. The yardsticks for goodness are very idealistic and out-of-reach, but the real problem is with the yardsticks for badness and the problem is that they focus on one aspect: violence, physical suffering and the taking of life. In that way they limit and sensationalize evil. We would find it more difficult to find unanimity on other aspects of badness, and also on less obvious examples of goodness. When there are collateral fatalities among civilians in a war, is that an example of evil or badness on the part of those responsible or not? Is it bad to amass a lot of wealth by lending money at exorbitant rates? Is it evil to destroy the careers and personal happiness of rivals to secure one's own advancement? And where do we situate these things on a scale of badness? And there could be many examples. Is it good to tell lies publicly, to put out false propaganda to justify some political action, like going to war against a dictator? Is it evil?

Is it the case that one can only appreciate the role of good and bad if the following conditions are met?

1. (however strange it may seem) you see them as both necessary in this life on earth,
2. you understand that just as an electron can be a wave or particle, a boson can be a fermion or a fermion a boson (see chapter 5), sometimes good can be bad and bad can be good, and
3. you agree to see life on earth and life after death as forming a whole, a continuum.

These three must be perceived as acting together; they cannot be experienced separately. Everything in our lives and on our earth is based on binary systems. Positive and negative, heat and cold, day and night, male and female. And of course, good and bad. You can't have one without the other. Different religions see evil and whatever is responsible for evil in different ways: the devil,

Satan, Lucifer. In Christianity the devil is a tempter but in Judaism for example the devil does not exist with that role nor is he depicted as something that should be fled from as in Islam. In Judaism Satan is not the opponent of God but a challenger who is there to make it more of a challenge to choose good. In that way Satan is a servant of God. This interpretation of the embodiment of evil, the devil, as part of the divine structure is possibly an important one. In Buddhism the 'evil one' is called *Mara*, and Mara tempts not only with material and sensuous pleasures but with riches, fame, power, honour, relief from hunger and thirst and so on. By the time we get to the date of The Tibetan Book of the Dead there are many evil and ugly spirits whose role is to tempt and frighten us – though the *Bardo Thötröl* makes clear that they are products of our own mind. In Hinduism there are many evil spirits, some worse than others, the most powerful being the *asuras*. But they should not be considered as fully evil or bad, probably just more evil than good, just as the Hindu gods are not always all that good – but the creator of all, *Brahman*, is beyond good and evil.

In one of his lectures Rudolf Steiner pointed out that we are two, and always binary. We have two hands, two eyes, two ears, two legs and we belong to two worlds. We are attracted by two forces, one of which is Lucifer and the other known as Ahriman. Lucifer is the force of evil that comes from within, our passions etc. Ahriman is the force of the external world, its riches etc. Man stands

> in the midst of a battle. A being from the left is fighting in man with a being from the right. If we were able to be entirely within our left half we would have a powerful perception of the one being, and if we were in our right half we would have a correspondingly powerful perception of the other being. Our existence as a double being arises from the fact that the Luciferic being is fighting in us from the left and the

Ahrimanic being from the right.
(Rudolf Steiner Archives, http://www.rsarchive.org)

Both of these forces possess positive and negative aspects. Usually we are taught to view Lucifer as the one who brought evil into the world. But he also brought freedom. And Ahriman may distract us with worldly goodies but this force has also brought progress in many domains, scientific, medical, technological. These figures are myths of course but like all myths they clothe certain realities, which are represented in different ways in different cultures. To dismiss them as mere fantasy and ignore them entirely would be to miss something important.

No consideration of good and bad, of good and evil, can ignore the content of the book of Genesis, common to Judaism and Christianity, accepted by Islam. The book of Genesis with its creation story and its tale of Adam and Eve is not of course to be taken literally but it does very seriously tell us many important things about the purpose of life and about our make-up. Max Heindel, the American Rosicrucian of the beginning of the 20th century, is a mine of information on this subject. Heindel reminds us that because of translation problems from the Hebrew there have been many things that are sometimes unclear in versions of the opening of the book of Genesis in many languages. Added to this is the certainty that, for those who wrote it, Genesis was not meant to be a book of popular science for the masses. And it should not be forgotten that we do not possess, as far as we know, the original texts; the texts we have are not earlier than the 10th century before Christ and the final form was not put together until as late as the 5th century BC.

There are two interpretations of the opening lines of Genesis and the second one is particularly relevant to this chapter. (It seems to be a question of translating from Hebrew and of presence or lack of vowels.) The first and generally accepted translation runs: 'In the beginning God created Heaven and earth.' In the second interpretation we have 'By means of the eternal essence of space, the double energy formed the double heaven.' God, the Creator, is thus seen as being double, of being positive and negative at once. The word *Elohim* in the first chapters of Genesis is usually made singular and translated by 'God'. But Elohim is plural and not only plural but masculine and feminine at the same time. And so, the Elohim, the gods of Genesis who did the actual creating, possessed both sexes. In the Cabbala the *Elohim* are the angels of the Archangel *Haniel* and belong to the sephira *Netzach* which is the sephira that rules creation and conception and gestation. Thus we are in a world of duality. Likewise it was not one man that was created but the human race – the plural form is used before Adam and Eve are even mentioned. The creation of Eve is not the creation of woman from a rib of Adam but the separation of the sexes – from double-sex, hermaphrodite beings we became male and female. Heindel argues that 'rib' is a mistranslation and should be 'side', meaning that the feminine side separated from the masculine side and the human race became divided into two sexes. (Always this duality…)

The stage is then set for the appearance of Lucifer. Lucifer is the name for the fallen angels who were unable to take a physical body of their own. But they were able to inhabit the brain of man. At that period of development of humanity, says Heindel, man was only vaguely aware of the physical world and it was through woman, who had a more developed Imagination (Heindel uses a capital letter), that the Luciferian angels were able to make mankind aware of how to create life just as the *Elohim* had done. Hence the myth of the famous apple. But in fact mankind found that while they could now create life, they had brought death within their world, and suffering as well. This situation led to the development of a greater ego-sense in mankind and parallel development of the intellect and of the possibility of choice. And this was the Original Sin. Mankind then had a choice of doing good or doing bad. Myth or not, this account tracks the moral development of mankind. This possibility of struggling between good and evil has been necessary for mankind. Rudolf Steiner approaches this issue in a series of his lectures where he talks of the role of Mikhael as being that of the archangel whose role it is to help man acquire the strength to lift himself out of the grasp of the Luciferian forces and with his own free-will become perfect like God. (A promise of the Psalms and also of Jesus Christ, see chapter 15.) And this struggle out of the Lucifer influences is to take place in our physical life in this world. Once again we see reference to the belief that we can only learn in this physical world, after death it will be too late. We are told also that after death, in a later stage of the afterlife, we will meet the Luciferic being again but this time he will have a different role, that of friend and ally. The negative role of Lucifer is operative only on this earth 'when we are entangled in earthly affairs'.

And enter the Cabbala. As illustrated on page 31 the Cabbala represents the different levels of being from the most subtle and spiritual to the most physical. Associated with each of those ten sephirot there is a negative force called a *klypha* (plural, *klyphot*) which means 'husk' or 'rind'.

They are concentrated in the *Olam Assiah*, the world of action, the one we live in, and are the waste matter and impurities left after the wave of creation has passed through the sephirot *Binah*, *Geburah* and *Hod*. As a negative force they operate therefore mainly in the world of matter and can be associated with catastrophes on the face of this planet among other things.

Some interpretations of the *klyphot* characterize them as the shadow of the ten sephirot; they would share the same structure but be invested with demonic powers which can corrupt our present universe. They have their origins in worlds that have disappeared before ours. But at the end of time, says the Zohar, they will be destroyed and transfigured into light.

So what is 'bad' is what is negative. But without it the positive would have no sense and no reason to exist. It is like anti-matter, often invisible, potentially destructive, all pervasive and inevitable, at least with the present structure of the universe.

What examples can we find of good and bad or good and evil? How can they be characterized in a useful way?

All of the major religions recognize that evil or bad exists and in general the forces that work evil are in some way inevitable, even necessary, and in some cases are explicitly at the service of the Creator(s). The Cabbala as usual puts in very succinctly in making evil a part of the world of *Malkhuth*, the lowest of the *sephirot*, which is not only our physical world but all of the forces (of electromagnetism for example) and the spirits that it contains. Seen from our human perspective many of these negative forces are seen as destructive and harmful but seen from a higher perspective the negative forces and the positive ones are seen as complementary. When we look at these positive and negative forces and events we can see them as falling into two classes:

1. The bad things that can happen to us human beings: illness, accidents, losing dear ones, unjust treatment, premature death, natural disasters like typhoons, floods, earthquakes, wars and so on
2. The bad things that we choose to do ourselves, to ourselves or to others

The big question is: have they the same cause? This may seem a foolish question but is it really? For it is asking whether in some way there is a relationship between how we behave and what happens in nature. It is worth remembering at this point that in all the eastern religions we are One with all things. We are inter-related. Science nowadays presents examples of this. The now famous 'Butterfly effect' describes how a small change in initial conditions can result in a huge change in conditions much further down the line so that the flap of a butterfly's wing in Costa Rica can cause a cyclone in Bangladesh. As James Gleick pointed out in his book *Chaos* popular wisdom has always been aware of this:

> For want of nail, the shoe was lost;
> For want of a shoe, the horse was lost;
> For want of a horse, the rider was lost;
> For want of a rider, the battle was lost;
> For want of a battle, the kingdom was lost!

And physicists will tell us that a change in the spin of an electron here beside us will cause a similar change in an electron at the other end of the universe...

> Quantum theory (...) reveals an essential interconnectedness of the universe. It shows that we cannot decompose the world into independently existing smallest units. As we penetrate into matter, we find that it is made of particles, but these are not the 'basic building blocks' in the sense of Democritus and Newton. They are merely idealisations which are useful from a practical point of view, but have no fundamental significance. In the words of Niels Bohr, 'Isolated particles are abstractions, their properties being definable and observable only through their interaction with other systems.'
> (Fritjof Capra, The Tao of Physics p 137)

In *The Tao of Physics* Capra went into considerable detail about this issue of non-local connections. He describes a ground-breaking experiment involving electron spin. Electrons do not spin like, say, tennis balls. The amount of electron spin is always the same. The electron can spin in one or the other direction, clockwise or anticlockwise of a given axis of rotation. Scientists use the terms 'up' and 'down' to refer to the two directions of spin. 'The crucial property of a spinning electron,' says Capra, 'is that its axis of rotation cannot always be defined with certainty.' But when a measurement can be performed 'the electron will be found to spin in one or the other direction about that axis'. Before you measure it, it merely 'has a tendency to spin about a definite axis'.

In the experiment which Capra describes two electrons are spinning in opposite directions and though their total spin is zero we do not know for certain the direction of the individual spins or the axis. The two electrons are then positioned at a greater or lesser distance from each other. I won't attempt to go into how this is set up! The important thing is that the distance between the particles can be small or large, even very large, one on the earth and the other on the moon. The observer now chooses a definite 'axis of rotation' for particle 1 and will obtain an 'indirect measurement' of the spin on particle 2 without approaching it. It is the interference of the experimenter that determines the axis rotation, previously uncertain, of particle 1. This can be done even when the particles are far apart. And in all cases, even when they are far apart, we find that particle 2 which may be many thousands of miles away, will also acquire a 'definite spin along the chosen axis', that is the axis of particle 1. There is no known way it could receive this information, which is 'transferred' at a speed faster even than the speed of light. Quantum scientists' explanation for this mystery is that the two particles are not separate but an indivisible whole.

So there is an overall Unity of everything which is exactly what the Vedas said. 'A true knowledge of the Unity of the Self begins by the perception of essential Unity – ONE matter, ONE life, ONE spirit, ONE soul in multiple forms' (Sri Aurobindo). But operating within that Unity is a whole system of binary opposites. They are the mechanical movements of reality as we know it. Beyond them, in the Unity, the opposites disappear. Evil and good are a feature of those opposites. And so the suffering that can happen to us, individually or collectively (in the case of natural disasters) can be linked, perhaps must be linked, to the pain or suffering we are responsible for. Put in another way and more dramatically, that the floods, typhoons and other natural disasters that confront humanity and cause millions of innocent deaths, are our own fault and a result of our human actions. And not only those actions that are linked to the preservation of the environment! It is all part of the mechanical movement of binary opposites that control our physical and psychic existence. So to return to the question at the beginning of this chapter, 'evil' is ignorance of the true Self, and it is part of the balance of life and death. This should not be read as an endorsement of evil. Hopefully suffering will decrease and disappear. The survey in this chapter seems to be saying that it depends on us.

The next chapter will continue exploring problems of good, evil and suffering. More particularly it will focus on a perspective from which evil loses its reality and its threat to our peace after our passage out of this life.

Chapter 14

A Learning Experience

Are good and evil the same thing?

Is it possible, as the last chapter seemed to hint, that we create our good and evil? That we are the creators of our own world and its difficulties, problems and sufferings, as well as its happiness? And that upon the quality of this creation of our life in the world the quality of our life after death will depend? These are the questions which this chapter will approach. So what if everything IS one WHOLE? There may exist a 'field' around us and in that field there may be positive and negative forces that are active, and which interact with each other in a creative way. Just as manure feeds plants perhaps the things we perceive as bad or even evil have a purpose in the larger scheme of things. A look at the ancient Hindu theory of *chakras* gives some food for thought. The *chakras* are vital energy centres in the human body, not unrelated to the Chinese theory of meridians. There are seven main *chakras* positioned as shown in the following diagram:

Sahasrara - the top of the head

Ajna - the forehead

Visudha - the throat

Anahatta - the region of the heart

Manipura - the navel and the solar plexus

Svadhistana - the sexual organs

Muladara - the base of the spinal cord

Figure 4: The Chakras

As can be seen *Sahasrara* is the most spiritual of the seven and the closest to the Self. *Muladara* is the most material. Putting it in very basic terms *Sahasrara* could be seen as associated with Good and *Muladara* with Evil. But, and this is important, it is *Muladara* that provides the raw energy that is transformed as it passes up through the *chakras* into a positive, creative force. At some point that energy becomes feelings, and then becomes thoughts.

Thoughts are creative. We can create our world and it can be good or bad.

A Bulgarian spiritual teacher who lived in France in the last century said to his disciples.

> Do you know that suffering was not given to mankind to make them suffer? The creator did not create suffering, it is we ourselves who have created it. (…) Suffering should not exist. It exists because something is not quite right with us. We learn through suffering, it makes sense, it's a way of rediscovering the right road and it's a blessing. When we find that road we will suffer no longer.

It is our thoughts, feelings and actions that create the world we live in. But this creation is unconscious and uncontrolled. Hence the suffering and the pain. The Psalms tell us, 'Know that you are Gods', and the Gospel of John says the same thing. Gods create worlds so man can also create in the same way for as Krishna put it in the Bhagavad-Gita: 'The splendour of light that comes from the sun, and which illumines the whole universe, the soft light of the moon, the brightness of fire – know that they all come from me.' And a man who reaches enlightenment becomes one with Brahman, the Creator: 'When he knows me in truth he enters my being.' We are then able to create consciously.

However, in our unconscious creativeness we can create negativity, pain and suffering.

Do you find it hard to swallow that we create worlds? But look around us. Couples create children, whole potential lives. A God-like act of creation which interestingly, involves the number 2, the two principles, the positive and the negative. People in depression create for themselves a world of misery. Human activity is destroying the ecological balance of the planet. CO_2 gases are causing global warming. Who is creating this, the Creator or us? It's always convenient to blame others. Consider the origins of the two great wars of the 20th century. They could have been avoided. But human stubbornness being what it is and an inability to foresee effects that should have been foreseen caused millions of deaths and immeasurable suffering. Is it idealistic to suggest that if heads of state had held to the Noble Eightfold Path of Buddhism, or the rules of other traditions, the worst could have been avoided? What we feel leads to what we think, which leads to what we do. In this way our personal lives are inseparable from the macrocosm. We are responsible for the realities we create. You may say we are not responsible for earthquakes and hurricanes. Well, natural disasters like that can be seen as the effects of the negative forces that work in our world but through our actions we create conditions which make them more likely and more deadly. And what if the negative actions performed in the world can have effects anywhere else on the planet?

In the world we live in right now there are certain acts of barbarity and cruelty that take place that are impossible to understand and terrible to even think about. I could unfortunately cite quite a number but will refer to only two, not probably among the best known. It has happened more than once in the past few years that paramilitaries in rural villages of Colombia, to punish people they believe of having collaborated with rebels (the FARC) take the suspects and, before the assembled villagers and families, to terrorise these into compliance, dismember the suspects live with a chain-saw, piece by piece. A second example, again I think not widely known, in a certain central Asian state the president, who has been in power there since Soviet times, has been known to execute political opponents by boiling them in oil. Such examples illustrate the degree of cruelty of which man is capable towards his fellow human beings. Many other examples exist. It is a fact also that in western Europe public executions by slow torture were not uncommon in the Middle ages and even much later.

How are we to explain such things? Mental unbalance on the part of the perpetrators? We can find similar cases in the history of serial killers and psychopathic murderers in our everyday criminal justice. But in the cases cited it is a feature of a kind of political intimidation, totally conscious and premeditated. It is like rape in war time. The only way to look at it is as part of what we have created jointly. We have by our behaviour created the earth in which these things can grow. And while this inflicting of suffering may be jointly created, it is at the same time the creator of further events yet to come about in the world. It is a vicious circle. It is the world of darkness, of *Tamas,* as the Vedas call it. The world of the *klyphot,* the negative sephirot of the Cabbala. A world where there is distortion of the mind and from which any kind of idealism or compassion is excluded. The Bhagavad-Gita attests to the existence of 'evil men who know not what should be done or what should not be done (...) these men of dead souls, of truly little intelligence, undertake their work of evil: they are the enemies of this fair world, working for its destruction.' The creator does not control everything. Nature is the source of all material things. The creator can only observe the work of nature.

Among Christians the best known example of suffering inflicted by his fellows on a man is, I suppose, the torture and crucifixion of Jesus of Nazareth. Mel Gibson's film on the Passion depicts the brutality of that story in gory detail. In order for that to happen there needed to be people prepared to carry it out and a reason. Looked at from an oriental viewpoint an interesting perspective is opened: what is the role of *karma,* in this event?

Those who condemned Jesus, who tortured him and eventually nailed him to a cross, were they doing their duty, their 'work' in the same way as Arjuna in the Bhagavad-Gita? I think the answer has to be yes. In the same way that Christians accept that it was the fate of Jesus to die on the cross, it was his *karma.* Or more exactly his role or his 'work' as the Gita puts it. Nature had so arranged things that all of that should happen and it was impossible to stop it. And it had a spiritual reason. In Christianity this was to cleanse mankind of its sins and provide proof of the Resurrection. Steiner has a slightly different perspective on it which is very relevant to what was put forward above regarding acts of wanton cruelty of man to man. For him a major mission of Jesus was to cleanse the earth of accumulated 'objective karma'. When a person performs a bad action he or she incurs personal karma for it which has to be compensated for some day. But the *emotional effect* of the action remains in the history of the earth and this is what Steiner calls the 'objective karma' that Jesus wiped clean. He was dealing, in other words, with the sins of the world, not with the sins or faults of the individual (which must be balanced some day by the individual). For example, a man put out the eyes of another in a former incarnation; this deed must be paid for in some way by the perpetrator, by suffering or by performing an equivalent good deed in a later life. And so the personal karma is balanced. But what of the very fact of that act of violence? The violence and suffering generated by it remain an objective fact in the history of the universe. We could say, I suppose, that the act of violence itself feeds the world of the *klyphot.* That was what Jesus redeemed according to Rudolf Steiner. Without this, according to Steiner, the earth, because of the accumulation of endless cruelty and lack of love would have been swamped by toxic effects. The further evolution of the earth itself, quite apart from that of humanity, would have been impossible. The earth itself has to evolve and develop just as we human beings do.

Looked at from these perspectives everything in our lives and in history follows a plan, and as long as we live in a physical world, in *Malkhuth*, the world of opposites and duality, we are made up of plus and minus symbols on a cosmic balance sheet that is both individual and collective. The day the pluses and minuses cancel themselves out we will have left the world of *Malkhuth* for a different and hopefully better place.

So why be good? 'For our own happiness and that of the world,' is the only sensible answer. Would we wish to end suffering, that of the world as well as our own and that of those near to us? Most people would say yes – if they take the time to reflect about it. But why, then, has the end of suffering not come about, at least of that suffering we are responsible for? Surely because there is constantly a conflict with our own interests. A glance at history books tells us that even our major religions have many times been guided more by their own interests than by compassion for fellow human beings. The road to the end of suffering may seem hopelessly long and it no doubt is. For the moment we seem in the sway of the negative forces that cause unhappiness and suffering. We are surrounded by wars, hunger, poverty. The Upanishad *Isha* stated that 'by life in the world you overcome death'. Life in the world means life with all that is evil as well as that which is good. And yet it is through that 'life in the world' that we can overcome death... Escaping from evil is possible only with Enlightenment. In the Upanishad *Brihadaranyaka* we find: 'He who knows the Self is unaffected, whether by good or by evil. Never do such thoughts come to him as "I have done an evil thing", or "I have done a good thing". Both good and evil he has transcended and he is therefore troubled no more by what he may or may not have done.'

Religions try to make the world a better place – at least some of the time. Christianity, Islam and Judaism teach compassion and generosity. Buddhist philosophy offers the Noble Eightfold Path, surely as simple a blueprint as you could wish for a happy and safe world:

Right understanding
Right thoughts
Right speech
Right action
Right livelihood
Right effort
Right mindfulness
Right concentration

But the effects of all of this have been limited, sadly. Perhaps, and it's a pessimistic position maybe, we must not lose sight of the fact that good and evil are the dynamos of our physical lives. Without them there would be no life as we know it and no development beyond what we are now. Oriental philosophies see life as something that continually evolves towards a distant perfection and seeing life as something that evolves towards some ideal completion explains many things. One day suffering will disappear. That will be when we no longer need it. For the moment it is present in our lives and around us and we need to understand it to try to better control it.

The question it is necessary to come back to is this one: Are good and evil in some way not only interconnected but something more than that? Seen from a distance are they the same thing? Is it just a question of perspective? Charles Morgan was an English novelist of the 1930s, never very well-known in his home country but appreciated on the continent. His novel *Sparkenbroke* tackles the moral issue of the good or the suffering we may be responsible for. And it is not simply a question of asking, 'If life is so short why should we burden ourselves with social rules that interfere with our happiness?' The question is, 'If, to experience transcendence and know Truth, we have to infringe moral rules, is that not justified?' And this is what the principal character of the novel believes. It is the story of an Englishman, an aristocrat and a poet, amoral in character but a mystic and an aesthete, and of his affair with the young wife of his best friend. But Piers Sparkenbroke is on a romantic quest for a perfection in death and love and in a mystical union of the two, something transcendental in which death is infused with a beauty not found in life. He and Mary, the wife of his best friend, become lovers. She too is drawn helplessly into this mystical passion and they eventually plan to run off together. But death, that they have been courting for a time, comes upon them and Sparkenbroke, in the evening when they were to leave together, dies of a heart problem. Mary tries to kill herself, fails and returns to her home and to her husband George. Everyone has suffered in this entangled love affair: Sparkenbroke and Mary, Sparkenbroke's wife and Mary's husband. In the minds of the lovers there is something they cannot control; there are two worlds, a normal world which is in their control and another world of passion which they cannot resist. The person I would wish to draw attention to is George, the country doctor, older than his wife, regular in habit, sober, well-balanced, but colourless beside Sparkenbroke. He is the person who should suffer most from this affair but it turns out to be a chance for him to know himself and to grow. And he achieves this calmness by continuing quietly to do his work as a doctor. And that is worth pondering: that the suffering that people cause can actually be helpful to those they cause it to. It is less likely that Sparkenbroke and Mary could have emerged from their emotional anguish with any greater clarity of mind.

Things would be incomplete without considering two other aspects of suffering. One is the suffering caused by natural disasters, floods, hurricanes and the like. And the other is the suffering caused by people acting through what they believe to be justifiable moral and religious reasons who bring death and destruction to innocent civilians. Examples of the second are not limited to the many latter-day terrorist attacks and suicide bombs. They can be found in many places in history. The persecution of the Cathars in southern France in the late 12th and early 13th century is just one example. The city of Béziers, to take just one example, was a place in which there were a number of 'heretics' but they were nevertheless a minority. However, the whole population was put to the sword – tens of thousands – with the justification that 'God will recognize his own'. The siege of Jerusalem by the crusaders in the 11th Century resulted in the murder of thousands of its innocent inhabitants of that city by the conquering crusaders. (I think cases like this are fundamentally different from vivisection in rural Colombia and boiling opponents in oil in Central Asia. The cases referred to now involve ideologies.)

There seems to a sort of gratuitous suffering in these cases. What to make of it? Are these cases like that of Arjuna in the Bhagavad-Gita whom Krishna told to carry on his fight as it was his *karma* and duty? Can one say that Arjuna's fight had a more idealistic cause than that of the crusaders? He like them accepted that he had to slaughter fellow human beings who were in the role of enemies. So probably not. The only key is provided by the concept of personal reward – even if it is reward in heaven. The noblemen who joined in the Crusades in Palestine or in the South of France did so for their own personal financial enrichment (mostly), though some, in the manner of the extremist Islamic terrorists of our day, did it in order to win Paradise. But in all of those cases the interest was purely personal and linked with what we have called the lower 'self'. Krishna, in the Bhagavad-Gita, makes clear that while Arjuna should continue the fight he must not consider the reward: 'Set thy heart upon the work, but never on its reward.'

So what makes the action evil can be seen as the degree of personal self-interest that is invested in it.

This leads to the other kind of suffering, that caused by

natural circumstances. Obviously there is no personal interest involved here except where the disaster is in some way provoked by the actions of man. But personal interest needs to transform itself into solidarity in these cases, a return to John Donne's well-known 'no man is an island'. In the oriental beliefs the Soul or Self is present in all things equally, our impression of being separate is an illusion; we are all one. Therefore the suffering of others is our suffering. In this way suffering especially that caused by natural disasters produces generosity and we see this at work in the many NGOs who spring into action following floods or earthquakes. So in a way we have a double test in these situations: a test of endurance for those who are the victims, and a test of unselfishness on the part of the helpers. It is a chance for the spiritual to be born out of the physical.

In our modern times an example of the combination of the spiritual and of life in the world, can be found in the work of the Ching Hai Association which has many tens of thousands of followers in East Asia particularly. It is a spiritual association, not professing any particular religious allegiance though accepting Ching Hai as a teacher, guru or Master. She is of Vietnamese origin and was brought up in a mixed Christian and Buddhist family. She spent years in meditation in Buddhist and Hindu monasteries and, as believed by all her followers, reached Enlightenment as a result. In spite of the very oriental nature of her practice she does not identify herself with any of the mainstream religions, even the eastern ones. The life of the spirit is central to the movement and all followers meditate for at least two and a half hours a day. But they also give themselves whole-heartedly to all kinds of relief work especially in south east Asia but in other places also, and Ching Hai and her followers have been tireless in the face of typhoons, floods, tsunamis. An example of putting into practice the belief that 'no man is an island', but also the lesson of the Upanishad *Isha* that 'by life in the world they overcome death, through meditation they achieve immortality'.

There is higher than reason (there is mind, spirit, soul) but reason is essential, and the Hindu scriptures make this clear. Reason is there to control passion for 'from passion comes confusion of mind, then loss of remembrance, the forgetting of duty; from this loss comes the ruin of reason, and the ruin of reason leads to destruction'. Destruction of what? Of the Self. Of the possibility of passing with full consciousness into life after death. It is a theme to be returned to in the final chapter but the message that comes across and through the varied belief systems is that the greater the level of consciousness one has at the moment of death the better. And that consciousness should be both of the good and the bad actions we have performed, not of the good alone. The last thing we want is to go through the process of dying in a mental torpor or even a lack of clarity.

One of the great messages of Hinduism is that all is One. We must not see each other as separate and individual, we are part of everything and everything and everyone is part of us. Whatever suffering (or happiness) there may be in the world it is a part of our greater nature. We may see it as objective but we should realize it is subjective.

Jalal-Ud-Din Rumi saw humanity as One. One of his poems tells of a man who was sent away from the door of a friend, a holy man, as being unworthy and who after a year of suffering (and purification) returned to his friend's house:

> From within his friend called out, 'Who's at the door?'
> He replied, 'It is you who are at the door, O charmer of hearts!'
> 'Since you are I,' the friend said, 'O you who are myself,
> Enter, there's no place in my house for two I's.
> (The Teaching of Rumi, Ed. A. Harvey)

The Christian Communion, as was pointed out earlier (see

chapter 8, pages 76-77) is a model of unity and Oneness. Saint Paul explicitly stresses that we are indivisible. Earlier in this book the concepts of 'personality' and 'individuality' were used to try to distinguish between the permanent and the changeable. But the individuality is also the Unity, the awareness of all being One. The individuality is the self and Self combined in a new way in which the consciousness that the self possesses is infused with the light of the greater Self and with an awareness of the unity of all beings. This unity with all beings, this awareness that we are not separate from our neighbours is a realization that is said to come to us in the period after death and this is approached in chapter 16. This vision of everything as One is not confined to religious writings or to saints. Walt Whitman is a well-known lay example of the praise of the One. And an atheist or at least agnostic French writer, Simone de Beauvoir, wrote in her Memoirs one day in southern Algeria near Nefta, in the Sahara desert:

> The sand-dunes undulated about me into the far distance, and I asked myself, 'Why is it so beautiful?' This endless sand gave me the feeling of a world that was smooth and safe, moulded from its surface down to its kernel in one single substance; a delicious play of curves and light emanated like music from the serenity of the One.
> (Simone de Beauvoir: Memoirs)

Religious writings, poets' insights, modern physics all point to the basic unity of all. If all is one, if I am all, and all is me, then I have every interest in doing good since to do harm is to hurt myself. From such a perspective evil no longer has a role to play.

And all of this is relevant to the effect on our deaths and whatever follows, of evil and suffering, of the bad we may do. Our lives are full of the temptation of self-gratification, self-interest. It is a desperate struggle to escape from this. But it is a learning experience and without it we would never have a chance of getting to a stage where we can create our own future consciously. So while it is often difficult to distinguish good from bad, because of the unforeseeable effects either may produce, they are both necessary – until such a time as they both disappear. For, if one disappears, the other must also disappear.

Of the two remaining chapters in this book the first will deal with the debilitating and negative effects of fear in our lives and how this is a handicap to our development after death. The final chapter will attempt to summarize the messages that the explorations in this book may have for us, and how they may make us feel more comfortable with the idea of death.

Chapter 15

The God Within

Pushing beyond fear

How many of us will admit that fear has a big place in our lives? A daily, persistent, never-ending fear of many things. All of us know someone who is prone to all sorts of phobias. But if we are honest and turn the focus towards ourselves we are not much better. Even if we consider that our fears are not full-blown phobias. Mostly, we would say, they are nothing but minor worries; they are there nevertheless. Illness or accidents, concerning ourselves or family. Gas leaks, fire, lightning. Burglars, muggings. An epidemic of avian flu. Growing old. Ferocious dogs. Drunk drivers. Plain drunks. Offending people unintentionally. Losing our passport when we travel. Unemployed immigrants. Other street-people. Strange noises in the night. A pain in the chest. A lump. Pollution. Pesticides and adulterated food. As well as fear for our material well-being, job, income, social standing. Not to mention fear of looking foolish, of saying something stupid. It is a shock to add up the number of fears and worries that take up space in our minds in each day we live. Anxiety is the number one disorder of our times. In the western world we are the leading consumers of tranquilizers. 'I'm worried about…' 'I can't stop thinking about…' How many times do we hear these introductory words in daily conversations? Just do a little eavesdropping in the tube, or the bus or train. The queue in a small-town post office is the unrivalled listening post for the world's phobias. Almost every conversation you may overhear will reflect some fear. Eckhart Tolle wrote a lot about what he called the 'body of suffering', which seems to correspond to what in the orient is known as the astral body, or more exactly the lower astral body. If we take no steps to counter it, it is the area of our psyche that has most control over our daily lives and a kind of control that can make a helpless slave of us. It is pre-eminently the dwelling-place of the self, the ego, the bit of us we know or think we know. It is the area where obsessions and rancour blossom, which our intellect or reason has great difficulty controlling. It is the area of unbridled imagination.

This imagination can be used to positive effect also. In ancient Rome and Greece the stoics developed a philosophy that was meant to cope with our fears. The idea was to train followers to not only imagine but live vividly in their imaginations the WORST that could happen to them, to live it FULLY in their imaginations and continually, so that they could be better prepared when it came about... One can understand how the stoics over the ages developed a reputation for pessimism!

Victims of our many fears, it is as if we are aware that life is by nature full of trials but we apprehend what those trials might be. The sages and *gurus* of all times have stressed that we are never given more trials than we can bear. In some cases this seems hard to believe when, thanks to modern communications, you are able to see the sufferings of various people on the surface of the globe in one catastrophe after another. The other thing the sages and *gurus* tell us is that 'this too will pass': nothing is lasting, things will change.

But it is still hard for us to escape from daily fears and anxiety. It is not easy to escape the lower astral and many people spend their lives there, in the turmoil of emotion, and not always turmoil, often simply confusion. A confusion of priorities, a refusal to see what is really important and an obsession with paying attention to what is in fact trivial. And often we KNOW that it is trivial but cannot help falling for it.

There are two places in the Bible where we are told that we are perfect, in fact that we are Gods. The first is in the Psalms. The Psalm 82 reminds us that we are in a mess, that we are in darkness, that everything in the world is out of tune and yet: 'I have said, Ye are Gods, and all of you are children of the Most High.' The second time is in the Gospel of John, when the conservative Jews are about to stone Jesus and he reminds them: 'Is it not written in your Law, I said, Ye are Gods?'

In the Cabbala, Malkhuth, this physical world we live in, is a direct reflection of Kether, the God-head, the Creator, Brahman, Allah... But the totally non-physical, spiritual essence which came from Kether has become more and more enveloped in denser material as it passes through the *sephirot* (or states of being), and from being non-matter, eternal and formless it has become a prisoner of matter and perishable. It is as if a mass of unobserved, indestructible particles from a non-material world that is invisible have gradually become the object of more and more observation and have become solid, yet ephemeral. But this is to paint only part of the picture. The earth is, if we are to believe what most spiritual teachers in an esoteric tradition have to tell us (and science also, it seems), is made up not only of the solid things we can see, but of a lot of subtler material. This subtler material is in the region where we find all the electromagnetic waves, where spirits of various kinds move, and the souls of those who die (for a time at least), as well as the souls of departed saints, the impulsions of the Christ Being, of the Buddha and Bodhisattvas, and Mohammed. The Psalms call this region of Malkhuth 'the land of the living' (see Psalm 116.9: 'I will walk before the Lord in the land of the living'). In fact the Cabbala teaches that there are seven levels to the Earth, seven states from the densest to the subtlest. In the same way that there are seven levels in man from the level of matter to the level of the spirit, the Self. It follows that through prayer or meditation we can rise up through the levels and reach the higher spiritual levels in ourselves and in the earth. And in this way we find the God existent outside us and the God within us. And the more we rise through the levels of being the more fear leaves us and peace enters us.

In Judaism the process of the creation of man is all the evidence needed for the eternal life of the soul and for the reality of the Creator within us. The Torah says, 'And the Almighty formed the man of dust from the ground, and He blew into his nostrils the SOUL of life.' The Zohar states that since God blew from within Himself, the human soul is therefore a part of God's essence. God is within us and since God's essence is completely spiritual and non-physical, it is impossible that the soul should die. For Jews this explains the words of King Solomon, 'The dust will return to the ground as it was, and the spirit will return to God who gave it.'

Deepak Chopra in his book *Life after Death* neatly paraphrases the teaching of the Vedas when he talks of the 'three states of consciousness' that represent all our experience:

1. The state of consciousness where we find material things
2. The state of consciousness where we find subtle things
3. The state of consciousness where there is only 'pure consciousness'

In the first state of consciousness we are in the physical, objective world that we can observe with our five senses and which exists in linear time. In this state certain Laws exist and they are strict: gravity, the speed of light, the conservation of energy etc. In the second state we are in the world of dreams, of imagination or creation. Laws are not strict here and time is not necessarily linear. In this state intuition rules, communication with the invisible world is possible and so is madness. In the third state we are above the ego and far from the body, the mind and the senses. This is pure consciousness, the kingdom of the Self, the 'always-so' of the Tao, or in the words of Saint John of the Cross:

I entered in, I know not where,

> And I remained, though knowing naught,
> Transcending knowledge with my thought.

This is the state where fusion of the soul and the Self takes place and where we can realize that God is within us. Of course this is a very difficult state to attain and no one denies that. It is the result of what may be years of practice and the reward of mystics and spiritual masters. But the possibility is there for all of us. It is the end of fear, the beginning of immortality.

Blaise Pascal, early 17th century French mathematician and religious thinker, said:

> The true and only virtue is, therefore, to hate ourselves (for our appetites make us hateful) and to look for a truly lovable being, in order to love him. But as we cannot love what is outside us, we must love a being that is within us and not ourselves, and this is true of each and every man. Now there is none like this except the Universal Being. The kingdom of God is within us, is ourselves, and is not ourselves.

'We cannot love what is outside us.' Because we do not truly KNOW anything that is not ourselves, we construct it according to our own selfish wishes, and so our love of things or people outside us is basically selfish and not love at all. There seems to me to be a great deal of concordance between Pascal's vision and the ideas of the Orient. What we have to hate, according to Pascal, is the part of us that seeks personal reward, personal pleasure and satisfaction. But there is something inside us that we can love, and that is the 'state of pure consciousness' that Chopra described. Inside ourselves we can find the vastness of space of 'the kingdom of God', in Pascal's words, the *dharmakaya*, in Hindu/Buddhist terms, endless space and timelessness. And 'this is true for each and every man'. No one can escape this responsibility: it must be faced sooner or later, in this life, in the afterlife or in a future life. All of this can be related closely to what we find in the Bhagavad-Gita and the Upanishads. 'Where is the Self? The sage replied: Within this body dwells the Self.' (Prasna Upanishad) 'When the mind of the Yogi is in harmony and finds rest in the Spirit within, all restless desires gone, then he is a Yukta, one in God. Then, his soul is a lamp whose light is steady, for it burns in a place where no winds come.' (Bhagavad-Gita)

In reaching this level of consciousness or something close to it not only fear, the everyday fears and phobias that all share, disappear, but also quite simply our attachment to the trivial and unimportant and temporary. As the Zen teacher said: 'Before enlightenment, carrying water, gathering wood, after enlightenment carrying water, gathering wood'. But in a different frame of mind.

It s important that fear should go out of our lives if we are to face death with any serenity. The Tibetan Book of the Dead presents us with the possibility of frightening visions in the period following death. But we are reassured to learn that these visions come from within us and cannot harm us. After some days the 'wrathful deities' appear to the dead person, drinking blood from human skulls and brandished knives, clubs and swords. The effect is meant to be terrifying and no doubt is. Chopra makes the point (In *Life after Death)* that the visions in the Tibetan Book of the Dead are those that belong to the Tibetan Buddhist tradition and that people of other traditions would see similar visions clothed in their own religious mythology. What is crucial, I think, is to notice that all these things come 'from within us'. In other words they are our creations. Deepak Chopra has also these significant words: 'The other worlds – in fact all worlds – are created in consciousness.'

Paul Brunton, in one of his books, asks the interesting question: 'Has anyone ever observed matter in itself, as apart from the objects in which it is supposed to clothe itself? Has it ever been accessible to the five senses of man?' He goes on to point out that apart from our perceptions there is no trace of anything we can call 'matter'. 'We can pick up no object, whether it be a stick or a stone, which is not picked up in conscious experience i.e. mentally.' From this mentalist position, which many would criticize, Brunton goes on to argue that it is untenable to think of matter and mind as being separate realities: the mind, an invisible reality which reacts to the visible one, matter. Matter is a product of mind; the world and everything in it is created by our minds. That does not mean it is non-existent, only that it is not real in the sense of having an objective 'reality'. What we see in front of us, a brick wall for example, is not deception, but 'that it exists around and outside our mind is deception'. We must bear in mind, says Brunton, that there is a vital difference between 'unreal' and 'non-existent'. Above all, and this is where his mentalism is interesting, we must not consider mind as being limited to the confines of our head. It is not, he says, limited to the physical brain but contains everything perceived and perceivable. The mind is 'dimensionless and measureless'.

This kind of thinking is echoed in Deepak Chopra's book on life after death. He refers to the 'field' in which everything is bathed. The universe contains 4% of all matter and energy which is visible and 96% which is invisible matter/energy. Between electrons, between all particles, between two ideas, between two moments there is always a space. This space is the 'field' and it would seem that we are all in some way connected to the same field of consciousness. In this field we can create everything we wish. Creation is a matter of projection from our consciousness. Our creations are often dependent on our culture so Christians – after death – create Heaven, angels, God and so on (as do Moslems and Jews), Hindus and Buddhists create *divas* and a pantheon of gods, *asuras* and *dakinis*. In this way we can transform what is unfamiliar into something familiar. In doing this we are in fact imitating the creator. We are stimulating the god within us. Of course the word 'god' here need not be taken to mean a single being, some would prefer to say 'gods' or 'spirit of creation' or 'creative principle'. But the fact is that this creative faculty is a key to our existence and comes from our consciousness, and it gives us all power for it frees us of time and space. We project ideas onto the physical world, our ideas form the existence of the world about us and this faculty of 'projection' from our consciousness makes us creators. It is now well-known in physics that the 'observer effect' actually creates matter. An observer is necessary to transform an invisible electron into a specific particle with its place in time and space.

In this way the fear of death which is one of the fears that people experience (though we usually don't consciously admit it) is unreasonable. (The question of fear AFTER death is something that will have its place in the discussion in the next and final chapter.)

We are in control after all, we are not mere puppets subject to the will of forces unknown to us. And of course the same applies to all of those fears we live with on a daily basis. They are negative projections created by our consciousness. Hence the continual emphasis in all religious and mystical writings on the importance of what the Buddhists would call 'right concentration' and 'right mindfulness', developed usually through the yoga of meditation. The reward of controlling the mind is freedom from fear and a realization of our power to be in command of our creations.

The Virgin Mary is of course revered as the mother of Jesus by all Christians and indeed also in the Koran. It cannot be without significance that in the Koran much more is made of Mary than of Jesus Christ and the immaculate conception is not at all disputed. Mary has a whole Sura that carries her name, Maryam, and it is one of the longer suras with almost one hundred verses. And Mary is mentioned elsewhere in the Moslem Holy Book. In the third Sura reference is made to aspects of Mary not mentioned in the Christian Gospels – at least in those we are familiar with. The birth and childhood of the Virgin Mary are mentioned. We see her mother praying for Allah's protection 'from Satan the outcast'. We see that Allah gave her health and 'goodly growth' and made Zachariah her guardian. Zachariah, whenever he went into the sanctuary (of the Temple) where Mary was dwelling, found that she always had food. Being asked where the food came from she replied: 'From Allah. Allah giveth without stint to whom he will.' Quite apart from the role of Mary in the Christian faith there is a piece of symbolism in the person of the Virgin Mary to which attention is not usually drawn. Mary stands for each one of us. What is the meaning of Mary, symbolically? Is it not that we all have God within us? This symbolism has often passed us by, yet it is full of meaning. God (the Creator, the spirit of creation) is within us. Says Svetasvatara: 'The truth is that you are always united with the Lord, but you must know this.' The food that is given to Mary in the Temple, can it refer to food that comes from her own Inner Self, from the God within her? One of the most beautiful, enlightening and yet mysterious paintings of Titian is the Presentation of the Virgin at the Temple. We see a young girl, in an aura of light, slowly climbing the steps of the Temple, towards Zachariah – presumably the same Zacharias, priest of the Temple, who was husband of Elisabeth, mother of John the Baptist.

Her mother and others are watching from the bottom of the steps; it is early morning. She is only half way up, isolated from and somehow different from all the other people below and above her, she is totally alone, but not afraid to go to the top. The light shining from within her shows that she need fear nothing: hunger, thirst or annihilation.

The fact that this symbol is a WOMAN says that in a sense we are all women. We all carry the embryo of God inside us, and we can all draw upon it for sustenance and growth. The Upanishad again: 'The Lord God, all-pervading and omnipresent, dwells in the heart of all beings. Full of grace, he ultimately gives liberation to all creatures by turning their faces toward himself.' (Svetasvatara)

Mary was not afraid to go the top of those steps. She felt no insecurity. She was secure in the knowledge that her God was not only with her but within her.

God is closer to man, says the Koran, than the vein in his neck.

Chapter 16

Going Beyond Repression

And seeing death as a different way of living

Fear can paralyze us, diminish our self-confidence, make it impossible for us to face the unknown and new. Self-interest, self-absorption lead us to concentrate on the personality and the impermanent and prevent us from being able to look beyond those. Being unable to concentrate fully on the present moment, being unconscious of our power to create our future, put us at the mercy of circumstances that, in our place, will decide our future. Being unaware of the role of good and evil in human existence makes us unable to transcend them.

The survey of the different belief systems and experiences related in the earlier chapters – Christianity, Islam, Hinduism, Buddhism, Judaism, the Cabbala and more – have been calling out to us that we must learn to distinguish the permanent from the impermanent, and that only in the permanent will we find the continuity of life after death. We need of course to refine our concept of 'permanence'. But most of us pay no attention to these calls. Maybe we should.

When we talk of 'the place of death in our lives', we need to look at it from two perspectives. It is, for example, the problem of coming to terms with the death of those dear to us. The first chapter discussed this in some detail and how we generally try to avoid the topic in modern, western cultures, until faced with it and even when we have to face it we still do all we can to avoid having to understand it in any way. And once the departed person is buried or cremated we more or less forget about death and get on with our lives. But the pain and feeling of absence are still there and can come to the surface unannounced along with the incomprehension, which is more a kind of deliberate freezing of our faculty of understanding. The second meaning of death in our lives is accepting our own death – the only thing we can be certain of, as someone said. There are many people who say: 'Well, we don't know what comes after, maybe something, maybe nothing; let's not concern ourselves with it but just deal with it when it comes.' In all our behaviour with regard to death we are engaging in a psychological repression of something we find unpleasant and incomprehensible. This is bound to create anxiety in us. Coming to terms with death and having a clearer idea of what it may mean will release this anxiety and can only improve our quality of life. Otherwise we can continue to bury our heads in the sand but nothing very constructive can come from that.

And what if there are some pressing reasons why we should be more aware of our future? What if this life and the next one are more intimately bound together than we imagine? What if the one prepares the other, this life on earth preparing the life after, and what if, as most oriental religions say, in the time between death and rebirth lies a period of preparation for another earth life? These are questions that, in a real sense, are vital and which call for answers. The answers are of course there but are not easy to come upon. They require looking into areas where scientific proof is not to be found. However the messages that come to us across the distilled wisdom of every earthly culture come to us in a quiet but persistent voice and in the end become a single message: that death is not an end but a beginning, that it is a different state that requires preparation, or a growth of awareness.

It is not that those messages tell us *everything* there is to know. You can know the position of an electron but if you know that, you cannot know the speed. Intelligence, the intellect, is an instrument for acquiring knowledge and it is a good one. But it has its limitations. It can prevent us from seeing other things. As philosophers like Karl Popper made clear, our knowledge advances by theories that are satisfactory for a time and then replaced by more valid theories. So truth is not set in stone. Medical research reported in this month's edition of the review *The Lancet* may be seen as ground-breaking, but in a year's time it may well prove to have been ill-founded. Intuition is another instrument for acquiring knowledge. It can be right and it can be wrong. It certainly needs refining. It has the advantage of being something that can be shared by more than one person. Clairvoyance is also a possible instrument of knowledge, a more difficult one to deal with because it is something that cannot be shared with another observer in the way a scientific experiment can be reported and replicated by peers. People who have claimed clairvoyance, such as Rudolf Steiner, or Max Heindel, the Rosicrucian, emphasize that clairvoyants can also be mistaken. Knowledge is gained gradually and can go through periods of observations that are incorrect and lead to erroneous conclusions. It is a bit like the voyages of discovery. Columbus thought he was crossing the ocean to reach Japan and China, countries described by Marco Polo who had approached them from the west. In fact, to his perplexity, he had found only an island evidently quite far from any mainland and inhabited by a race totally unlike the Orientals. He had difficulty understanding where he was. Even four voyages did not totally resolve the problem. The existence or extent of the continent of America was not immediately apparent to those early explorers. Another, perhaps less widely known, example is our knowledge of the River Niger. At the beginning of the 19th century little was known about the Niger, in which direction it flowed, where the source was to be found, and where it flowed into the sea (if not into an inland lake). Some thought the Niger was connected to the Nile, others that the Rivers Senegal and Gambia were its mouths. The uncertainties lasted some time. It took three European expeditions over a period of thirty years to answer these questions. Exploring the invisible world can lead to knowledge which is similarly incomplete or erroneous, and it is important to remember this. There is a vastness in the infinity of the invisible world that cannot be easily grasped by the limited mental faculties we use. This is something that we have to learn to accept.

Death is a feature of the physical world and observation shows without any doubt that in every case of death in nature we are looking at a change of form in the thing that has died. But: 'If any man thinks he slays, and if another thinks he is slain, neither knows the way of truth. The Eternal in man cannot kill: the Eternal in man cannot die'. (Bhagavad-Gita) The atoms that constituted the thing that has died do not die; they continue to form something else.

'It was when intelligence and knowledge appeared, that the Great Artifice began.' We read this in Lao Zi. But what are we to make of it? We can deduce that there was a period when there was not the 'Great Artifice' and a period when it began. That 'intelligence and knowledge' played a role in this beginning. But what is meant by 'intelligence and knowledge', what was the situation before, and, of course, what is meant by 'the Great Artifice'? We can deduce that 'intelligence and knowledge' are attributes of our intellect and that the intellect has created the Great Artifice. And the strong implication is that the Great Artifice is something we would be better without. The Great Artifice is everything that stands between us and a true appreciation of reality. It could then be compared to the daylight blue sky that masks the whole universe. When we were in intellectual darkness we could see the secrets of the heavens, is that what Lao Zi is saying? As always things are binary, a positive side and a negative side. Darkness here means light there. Heat in this part of the globe means cold in another. It is part of the Great Artifice to ensure that we see death and decomposition as being the end. We have all been struck at the sight of a departed family member lying in a coffin or on a bed and we have all felt painfully how everything we knew to be the person is no longer there. Whatever it was that gave life to that body is no longer there. It could be said that what has gone is a quantity of energy, the energy that gave the body life. When a body is burnt only some cinders are left, the rest has gone up in the flames: the 'rest' was also energy and it has disappeared from our physical field. The big question for most of us is: when that energy leaves the body does it have consciousness? Does consciousness end with death just as the physical body seems to end? Appearances lead us to believe that it does, but the quiet, persistent voice of the wisdom of mankind through the ages and perhaps a quiet persistent echo from deep within us says the opposite.

And we are led to consider death, as we observe it, as a feature of only the physical universe, but a feature which does not impact on things not physical, like consciousness. Then, taking this to be the case, we are forced to try to get some idea of how the life we lead on earth may interconnect with this afterlife. And lastly we must ask ourselves: how can we be better prepared for our encounter with death?

Death is something that is above all INVISIBLE and more so any afterlife that may follow it. We are not very good at handling things that are invisible. The issue of visibility and invisibility is not as simple as it may look. Take sound waves for example or indeed any kind of electromagnetic wave (outside the visible spectrum of colours). They are not visible to the eye but no one disputes their existence. A more subtle case is to be found in science. There are things in science that scientists accept as real but which they have never seen. You cannot see a virus with the naked eye or even with a microscope. Yet researchers routinely isolate and describe viruses. An astronomer who describes a galaxy not visible to the eye even with a telescope has no problem accepting its reality. But to accept that reality one piece of evidence is not enough, he needs to have evidence across a period of time. One sole image of a galaxy will not be enough to convince an astronomer. He will need several, with different wavelengths and treated in different ways as well as being spread out in time. The new phenomenon is not in the image but in an accumulation of factors of stability across a number of images. One sighting alone is not enough. One image itself in other words is nothing.

And so we spend a lot, of time, ingenuity and money making the invisible visible. By means of telescopes, electron microscopes, and so on. There are still things that we accept but which are invisible, like black holes or viruses. We have to rely on indirect means to 'see' them. When it comes to death and dying, however, we seem to be lacking the instruments. But there are some indirect means that we can use. The Cabbala comes to our help again for it represents all that exists, the visible and the invisible. Looking at fig. 1 (page 31, chapter 3) it is clear that the only VISIBLE world is *Malkhuth*. The invisible stretches from *Yesod* – which is the world of emotions, and our emotions are invisible – up through *Hod*, the intellect, and *Netzach*, the appreciation of harmony and beauty, *Tipheret*, love of mankind, and so on, up to the level of pure consciousness, the *always-so* of the Tao. The Cabbala makes a clear statement that the invisible exists and not only that it exists but that it is vaster than the visible. There is a parallel with the electromagnetic spectrum. Only a tiny part of the electromagnetic spectrum is visible to us as light, the rest is invisible. And so we can look upon the passage from life to death as a passage from a life in a visible, physical world to a life in a non-physical world invisible to our normal sight. There are cases, of course, as we all know, where that invisible world becomes in a certain sense 'visible' or perceptible.

When we look at the different accounts of people who say they can communicate with the dead or of those who have had Near Death Experiences, we find that the major religions do not seem to be talking in an arbitrary way although the picture they present may be incomplete.

Although an archbishop in the Episcopalian Church of the USA, James Pike admitted to not being a total believer, at least in the orthodox sense. He lost a son who killed himself in his early twenties after a short but difficult life of recurrent depression, aimlessness and drugs. Pike decided to consult a medium and was able to establish what seemed to be communication with his son, Jim. In addition, one of his assistants, a woman he calls Maren, was even less a firm believer than he, and, like Jim, suddenly ended her own life. She also seemed to talk to him through the same medium, and assure him that there was indeed a life after death. Pike was surprised when Maren told him that she and his son had met and that they lived now in 'etheric' bodies. Not a very conventional believer in her lifetime, she said also that she had been told that one day she would meet Jesus. She tells Pike that their present state is a temporary one and that souls move into higher worlds but sometimes also return to the etheric world – the immediately post-death world – to help others. Consciousness seems to survive according to this experience but Pike admits that we do not know if this first stage after death in which the dead person seems to have the same personality, memories etc as when alive is simply a survival of the energies that the person or persons had generated when alive, combined with unconscious mental images in the mind of the person receiving the message. In the world of nature, which is also our world, the death of everything is gradual, all change is gradual and it would be an exception to the general laws if change was SUDDEN and TOTAL. (So certain energies live on for a while after death like *footprints*.) In an earlier séance Pike is told by his son that he has been given a job to do which is to help suicides adapt to life after death. Rudolf Steiner also talks of how the departed are given tasks to do during the period in *kama loca* (see below), which resembles suspiciously the 'etheric' world referred to by Pike's son. Steiner even talks about people after death who are given unpleasant tasks to perform such as helping to engineer illness, accidents and natural disasters, as part of their karma generated on earth. To what extent is there 'learning' after death? Jim, Pike's son, tells his father that he has had to put away his 'diplomas' and see things again. He is, he says, living a 'new religion', but in which God or Jesus are not compulsory. A religion in which identification with others is the key, compassion, charity, mutual help are truly practised and a source of happiness. It is relevant to this that Steiner often makes the point that we cannot learn anything new after death, learning takes place in this life on earth. What this means may be that in order to understand life after death we need to possess certain concepts that can only be developed during physical life. Armed with those concepts we can understand what we see and hear when we leave the physical body with its physical senses, bearing in mind that 'see' and 'hear' do not have the same meaning here as in our material world. Are we not reminded here of the boat that Utnapishtim in ancient Babylon was instructed to build, the boat that would guarantee him immortality?

A.P. Sinnett, in an old but very informative book, spends a lot of time relating what oriental teachings say about *kama loca,* the period which follows death. It comes over as an intermediate period, a period of gradual, even very gradual separation from what we knew on earth. We are able to review our last life on earth, slowly rid ourselves of our passions and longings. In the *kama loca* period, Sinnett tells us, medium-derived experiences are possible but so is contact with the astral 'shell' of the departed which is therefore a mistaken kind of mediumship. It is possible to confuse the two, the real and the false. 'The entity has vivid consciousness of one sort or another over the whole time (in *kama loca*),' says Sinnett. The 'footprint', however, is also around and can be contacted. But as time passes the *kama loca* resident gradually loses touch with the earth. It is like emigrating to a new country; at first you feel a pull towards all that was familiar and even dear to you in your old country but as the years pass the memories become faded and the attachments loosen. You perhaps even begin to wonder how you were so attached to those now distant things. When contact with the earth is slowly lost a period then begins when one has visions simultaneously on all sides, when one feels oneself to be spread out in all space and one sees sights that one has never seen before – this resembles what is described in The Tibetan Book of the Dead (see chapter 2).

Several of our sources allow us a glimpse of some of the characteristics of consciousness after death. A lot of the serenity that one may or may not experience after death, we are told, is dependent on the quality of our life on the earth. The world after death is very different; it does not contain the same sense objects that we are used to. We do not have the same organs of perception. For anything to happen or be perceived by us in that state there must be absolute calmness of soul; it is impossible to activate oneself to gain information or knowledge. One has to wait in the same way that a poet or musician waits for inspiration. What have been during life our inner thoughts and feelings become our external world. 'After death all our thoughts and mental representations appear as a mighty panorama before the soul,' says Steiner. It would seem plausible therefore that the more dependent one has been in life on the sense organs the less prepared one is likely to be for the change. For example, we can meet someone we knew after death (that person may be still living or may be dead also) but it is a vision that is based on the affection or otherwise we felt towards the person on earth. We cannot develop this further. Particularly if our life with the person or persons had no spiritual content on earth. At least this is what Steiner tells us and he gives a poignant example. It is of a man who died prematurely leaving his wife and young children to whom he was deeply attached and with whom he had spent the happiest times of this life. In his afterlife he experienced great loneliness and an inability to connect with his family despite all his love and positive feelings. A situation due to the absence of any spiritual content in the relationship he had with his family on earth. 'Souls dwelling in the physical body must learn the language of the spirit,' says Steiner. 'We must acquire a knowledge of the higher worlds here (on earth).' How what we do on earth translates into the language of the other world is not as obvious as it might be thought to be. The language, or the mathematics, of the spirit are different.

Which brings us back to coming to terms with death and the story of Gilgamesh and the boat (see chapter 7). Utnapishtim's boat was a vehicle for crossing from life to death. It had to be constructed according to very precise specifications. The boat was, in other words, a kind of non-physical body. And this non-physical body had developed concepts adapted to a non-physical world. In this way it allowed a human to go through death with consciousness. Saint Paul called it the 'spiritual body', the Upanishads call it the 'Self', we can call it the 'soul'. It seems to be the case that it is by gradually awakening this body, through meditation usually or some form of yoga, that we can prepare ourselves for the change of state that occurs on our death.

There exist many accounts of people who go through Near Death Experiences (NDEs) during which a person, perhaps in an intensive care unit, undergoing surgery as a result of a violent road accident, or a victim of cardiac arrest, goes into a state that resembles death. The heart stops and the encephalogram may be flat. After a period of time, short or long, in this state they come back to life and are able to describe the experience. While there are individual differences in these experiences there are many common points. From what such people tell us after they have 'come back':

1. they experienced an intense feeling of peace

2. they saw their body from outside and from above
3. they felt no pain, even if the body they could see had multiple injuries (as a result perhaps of a accident)
4. their thinking was very rapid and clear
5. they had a new sense of time and space for time and space as we know them no longer existed
6. many also report that they felt themselves to be in a dark tunnel full of mist, heading towards a bright light at the end of it
7. some report that they saw the panorama of their past lives
8. there are also reports of negative experiences: extreme fear, feelings of isolation, guilt, torment, confusion. These appear to be small in number. They are interesting, however, for one can wonder whether they are a result of the continual repression of any consideration of death during one's life. In the same way one can wonder whether the dark tunnel and the mist described in many accounts is due to an absence of the concepts needed to comprehend non-physical life: that they had not developed 'a knowledge of the higher worlds while here on earth'.

There are differences from person to person due to the fact that it is our consciousness that creates these realities (cf. The Tibetan Book of the Dead). But there is a realization that this phase is transitory, and is not the end of the story. It is a road to something else. Certainly the thousands of documented NDEs challenge our orthodox western thinking on death and its aftermath. A frequent topic for debate is whether consciousness is dependent on the physical brain. 'Consciousness' (existing independently of any physical/material basis) is something that is not likely to be recognized by science. But the work of a cardiologist, Pim van Lommel, who has led research on NDEs provides some support for the idea. His article describing his 13-year study in ten Dutch hospitals was published in *The Lancet* in 2001. He examined 344 patients and found that they all shared a similar characteristic: that they had full consciousness during their NDE though instruments indicated that all cerebral activity had ceased. Not only were they conscious, but the field of their consciousness was vaster than ever. They could think very clearly and their memories could go back to their early childhood. What if, to return to a question already discussed (see pp 165-166), consciousness is not situated in the brain? What if it is embedded in a general 'field' in which we all swim like so many fishes? Deepak Chopra points out that this is compatible with all of the teachings of the Vedanta. It can be found in other religious texts also. For example, Saint Paul speaks of everyone, Jews or gentiles being 'in one body'. Likewise, the whirling dervish dances can be seen as a means of reaching this supraconsciousness, something Jalal-Ud-Din Rumi speaks of more than once. NDEs would be a 'stage in life after death which is still dominated by our memories and our expectations'. *Kama loca,* in other words, or the 'etheric' world described by Pike's son, Jim.

Steiner and Sinnett and others, including those who have examined NDEs, have tried to give us an idea of the sequence of events after death. The Tibetan Book of the Dead does the same thing within the Tibetan Buddhist culture. A number of spiritual teachers have spoken of the possible dangers for the departed when we try to evoke them in séances or otherwise, in that it may distract them from their progress in the afterlife. The majority of humans, says Mikhael Aivanhov for example, are not immediately freed of their earthly attachments, they continue to be bound to their relatives, friends, and even enemies, as well as to familiar places. And, unless they have some spiritual longing they may continue for a considerable time to hover around those familiar people and places. Contact can be made with these souls but it is not going to be very fruitful for either the departed or the living. And often the contact is with 'shells' or vibrations – 'footprints' – of the departed rather than with the actual soul.

The Tibetan Book of the Dead also says that after death the departed sees family and others and notices that 'his eating implements have been removed'. But, says Aivanhov, those who have brought a spiritual content into their lives are able to leave the physical world quite quickly. In many cases 'from the moment of their death, they are very far from the world, and they do not return towards it'. Rudolf Steiner created a prayer for the departed which emphasizes binding our thoughts and our love to them and sending them light and encouragement to progress on and on. It is in no way an attempt to bring their presence back to their earthly life. In fact, if we are to accept what Steiner says, the soul in the period after death is not interested in current happenings on earth but more engaged in a contemplation of his or her past life. 'We live with those individuals who are also dwelling in the spiritual world after death', in other words with the dead friends and relatives who have preceded us. We have little interest in those on earth. 'Only when those on earth seek us with their souls can a link with them be created' (the aim of Steiner's prayer). When we feel love and enduring sympathy for the dead, connections are made. If we forget them they forget us. There lies the importance of the tradition of commemorating the dead in all human societies.

We must therefore constantly bear in mind that the spiritual world has got to be very different from what we are used to on earth. There we are not contained in a physical body with five senses: we feel ourselves to be the whole of space, spread out in space. We are not able to 'localize' ourselves, there is no 'here' and 'there'. This means that we become, maybe gradually, part of the ALL. In such a way that we would become less and less individual and become more and more part of the 'always-so', of a broader consciousness. Connections therefore might not be simply a question of a communication between the departed and those left behind but of 'the departed + the ALL' and those left behind. Or 'the departed + x', x being other beings or existences with which the departed has become united.

We can find the account of the visit to Jesus of Nicodemus, a leading Jewish Pharisee, in the Gospel of Saint John. Nicodemus wishes to know how one can be 'born again'. Interestingly the word resurrection is not mentioned once, nor is there any reference to 'afterlife'. But the term 'kingdom of God' occurs more than once. 'Except a man be born again he cannot see the kingdom of God.' 'Except a man be born of water and of the spirit he cannot enter the kingdom of God.' 'Being born again' has to mean being born in a different kind of body with new sense organs, that enable man to see into the higher worlds, the world of *Devachan* in Hindu/Buddhist terminology (see chapter 2, page 26). It is the 'Kingdom of God', the world in which Utnapishtim was allowed to live and the world Gilgamesh wanted to live in (see chapter 7). To live there we must be able to see through the Great Artifice. To use terms from the Upanishads it must mean being born to the Self. Jesus tells Nicodemus: 'That which is born of the flesh is flesh; and that which is born of the Spirit is spirit.' What is born of the Spirit comes out of eternity and goes into eternity. 'The wind bloweth where it listeth, and thou hearest the sound thereof, but canst not tell whence it cometh, and whither it goeth; so is everyone that is born of the Spirit.' It is striking how these different sources often seem to be talking about the same thing, the Self or the Soul.

But being born to this higher Self does not mean abandoning the physical world. The physical world is the instrument we need in order to reach our Self, and despite the Great Artifice it must not be despised: it is our place of learning. As the Cabbala teaches, the world of *Malkhuth* is every bit as divine as the world of *Kether*. Jesus tells Nicodemus that to see the kingdom of God we must be born again 'of water and of the Spirit'. But where can a man be born again, go through the gestation period necessary for a birth? Only through the physical world we live in. The 'water and the Spirit' are to be found in that world. For some thinkers water represents universal, disinterested love and the Spirit is wisdom, the 'wisdom that passeth understanding'.

Love, disinterested love, is something we can only develop on earth; it cannot be developed after death and this can lead apparently to situations of great frustration in the spirit of a departed soul. Several sources indicate that when, after death, we spend a period reviewing our past life we will see again situations in which we have caused hurt but this time we will FEEL the hurt as if we were the person who had suffered it. This leads us to a realization that we are all one, of Unity. In the same way wisdom or knowledge can be developed as forms of action in this material world only, which means that in the after-life one can find oneself totally at a loss to understand anything of what is happening if we do not possess those concepts as forms of action All part of building the boat…

When we depart this body at death we enter the so-called astral world ('etheric' world, *kama loca)*. This can be a dangerous place and we no longer have the protection of our physical body which we are accustomed to hurrying back to for refuge when we have a nightmare. This is another reason why it is essential to become aware of what happens at death. A lack of preparation can mean a life in the after-death astral period where there is not only fear but also desperate loneliness. In terms that Steiner uses, it is possible for a person to become a kind of 'hermit' in that world. A person who lacked a 'moral disposition of soul' in life, who lacked care for others and an interest in others finds it very difficult, even impossible, to live with others in the after-life. The result is dreadful and excruciating loneliness. A person who goes through death in an unconscious torpor (this does not mean in a coma) misses all the valuable opportunities for learning and developing that are offered by the passage from physical life to death. The importance and the reasons of being conscious at the moment of death have been underlined more than once in earlier chapters. Without that consciousness the whole experience becomes similar to a dream that one cannot fully remember and which fades into oblivion. If the whole purpose of the exercise is to change and develop and learn, then a lot is lost.

From Pim van Lommel's observations it would seem that memories live on after death though our brain seems to have ceased functioning. How can this be so? Is it a further indication of the existence of a 'field' common to all things (see page 166, chapter 15). A field not dependent on the physical world. This field of consciousness common to all is a space where we can create what we wish. This is the realm of the creativeness of the spirit. Christians therefore create their Heaven, Moslems create their paradise, Tantric Buddhists from Tibet create their world of bodhisattvas and demons. The field allows us to make the unfamiliar familiar and this is of great importance in the early stages of a life after death, so we are told. In that existence we are multidimensional, we are freed from the fetters of time and space, our imagination and inventiveness know no bounds. Consciousness in these circumstances is indispensable…

'The sage,' says Lao Zi, 'takes this but rejects that.' The sage chooses, the sage exercises discrimination. When it comes to accepting the possibility of an afterlife what do we do usually? Some of us refuse the idea as pure fantasy. That is acceptable. It is a choice made. But many of us simply abstain, we do not take a decision, we decide to wait and see. And there is the problem. We do not make a choice. But in a way it is too easy to abstain. Is the problem that in accepting an afterlife new responsibilities are created which we would rather do without? Whatever the case, even on a common sense basis, life in a broad sense cannot end with the death of the physical body. All religious traditions and all the parallel systems we have looked at say that consciousness continues, and even sceptics looking at NDEs admitted things that science could not explain. The most striking thing, yet generally unnoticed, is the fact that nothing in nature changes abruptly, even the decomposition of the atoms making up our body is gradual and takes a considerable time. And so what of our consciousness? What of the 'field' that our consciousness seems to live in? It is as if we refuse to look at the evidence, to weigh the probabilities, as if we are in denial when it comes to looking at the passage from life to death. But is there not an urgent need for us to take the death-event and the death-state more seriously and to give them a place in our lives? We need to be more aware of it; it is nonsensical to simply wait and find out.

So there is a state that we enter after death. How can we get there safely? Every known religion or faith has a place for meditation or prayer. And every faith has a place for spiritual retreats that provide opportunities for some sustained prayer or meditation. In every case it is a matter of connecting to what we see as God. It is a way of establishing a harmony between ourselves and the cosmos, to put it as neutrally as possible. And it is important to realize that this need not be based in any religion. Religions have provided certain tools, prayer, meditation, fasting, and yoga, which are available for our use. But instead of connecting to 'God' we can try to connect to what is permanent within us, to the invisible 'boat' we need to construct. So it does not have to be a recital of fixed prayers, above all it is a connecting with the permanent and the invisible and a moving away from the smaller self. If this brings us the calm and peace we long for we have aimed well. The practice of meditation of any kind is a way of trying to get closer to the soul, or to the Self. It has proved to many of us that it can enrich our lives and reduce those fears that constantly haunt us, and prevent us from calmly seeing reality. It is a practice that strengthens the will. *Chandogya*, the Upanishad, reminds us that 'A man is above all his will; as is his will in this life, so does he become when he departs from it'. Creating an awareness of death is also necessary in the actual living of our lives. That other Upanishad, *Isha*, warns that it is fatal to devote oneself exclusively either to life in the world or to mediation. Buddhism stresses the importance in life of sociability, of keeping good company. Other religions make the same point and, while some do tolerate hermits and anchorites, they always stress the importance of life in society and of our duties with regard to our fellow human beings. In a sense the afterlife is a reflection of our current life!

Perhaps, at some point in our evolution, as Lao Zi suggests with his allusion to the Great Artifice, we possessed faculties of intuition that were reliable. That we were part of the Unity – *vidya* – but that at a certain time we lost those faculties and came under the control of *maya* losing our sense of the Unity – prisoners of *avidya* (the contrary of *vidya*). If that is the case we need to find ways of getting through that *maya*, of piercing the Great Artifice. In order to see things again as they really are we need to recapture a vision of the Unity of all being, including the unity of life and death. We need to develop new concepts about the nature of life and death. In particular we need to begin to see our own life-death as a continuum, and in general to see death as existing parallel to life. The Great Artifice has made us see life as something separate from death. We have become accustomed to see life as a state and death as an event. But we need to give them the same nature as states. There are always similarities between the way things happen in our daily lives and the way things happen in the life-death continuum. In our lives we prepare for exams, for job interviews, for important meetings and events. To engage in these events with success we have certain strategies that we follow. We do not only make practical preparations, we also prepare ourselves mentally. So that we are not unhinged, or destabilized by the event. We imagine it, we live it in our heads. Think of the stoics who trained themselves to live all kinds of disasters in their imaginations so as to be better able to cope with them. What if it is the same when it comes to the life-death continuum? We need to try to come to see birth and death and the life between and after as forming a whole. Or, as the sub-title of this chapter suggests, we need to see death as a different way of living. We have got into the habit of thinking that life and death are two separate things. We live our life – stage 1 – and when that stage is finished we die – stage 2. In other words they are arranged in linear time. But surely it is not like that. Life and death co-exist in the same time. Every instant something dies and something is born. In the world around us but also within ourselves. Parts of us die all the time and are replaced by new parts. The air we breathe dies when we inhale it, the food we eat dies. Our blood 'dies' in circulating and is revivified. So dying is intimately a part of living. It is useful for us to constantly remind ourselves of those things.

The explorations in this book tell us also that we need to be aware that it is important that we do not go through the gate of death in a torpor (we should exclude the state of being in a coma for in a coma there may well be another kind of consciousness). And we need to help those dear to us to be aware of this. Ensuring such a state of consciousness seems to depend on its cultivation during one's life. By making it part of our thoughts, reflecting regularly on it, and, if we are so inclined, through yoga or meditation. Focusing on the present moment is part of this – because day-dreaming leads to unconsciousness. Without this training one risks going into death in a dream. And that is what we want to avoid.

There is a serious risk that we have been neglecting those who have passed on ahead of us. We bury them and get on with our business. But it would look as if we should be doing something to help them, or to maintain some sort of contact. We should develop the habit of trying to reach them, particularly the very recently deceased, to send our thoughts to them, to send colours, like blue, to tell them not to fear any unfamiliar sights they may see or sounds they may hear; that nothing can hurt them, that everything comes from within themselves, that they should go towards the brightest lights, that they should not waste time looking backwards.

In this way we would train ourselves to see death and the dead as co-existing with life.

Our daily lives tend to whirl past us in a hurly-burly of tasks, we do not have the time to look at our lives objectively, to look at life and death objectively. We fear death, whether we admit it or not, as we fear anything we do not know and are not familiar with. For our own good, for our safe passage over the threshold between life and death we need to constantly be aware:

1. of the unreality of impermanence and the reality of an underlying permanence
2. of the fact that there is an invisible world that exists alongside the visible one and is much bigger
3. that our consciousness can survive death
4. that the dead have not departed completely and are close to us and that they depend on us and we on them.

Through daily awareness-raising we should gradually come to terms with death and ease the unconscious fears. We will then manage to resolve the internal conflict hidden within us, the refusal to face death, the repression of something too painful to acknowledge. Anxiety and fear, like those which haunt the agoraphobic and cut him or her off from the outer world, are what prevent us emerging from our limited self, our so fragile personality, and from seeing things calmly so that in that calmness we may see that there is more to life and death than we think.

It is clear that death is put there as a challenge. It is something we have to face and overcome. And overcoming it means going beyond our self-interest, our petty preoccupations. It means not focussing on riches or poverty, on comfort or discomfort, on praise or blame, on fame or obscurity. Put simply it means not putting oneself first, but giving of oneself, being aware that we are all one, not looking solely to personal satisfaction. Gilgamesh failed to achieve immortality for he could not stay awake six days and seven nights. He had not become aware of his higher Self which is tireless and needs no sleep. He was bound by his physical needs, his motives were selfish. He was never given the instructions for the boat. We, in our epoch, with our growing awareness of our common humanity, can find them, those instructions, scattered here and there in incomplete pieces, in unexpected places. Waiting to be put together.

Notes

Introduction

1. Samuel Taylor Coleridge in a letter

Chapter 1 The Storytellers

1. Mikhael Aivanhov, 1900–1986

Chapter 2 Beginners

1. The oriental theory that everything has an effect, good or bad, on our lives in this life or a future life.
2. Contrary to common belief, Buddhism does not deny the existence of a soul. It denies the reality of a 'personality'; the 'I' of one birth cannot be the same as the 'I' of a previous birth. But there is an *individuality,* a vital energy coming out of nirvana, that progresses through successive incarnations to become a Buddha.

Chapter 5 The Veil of Illusion

1. I am not a specialist in these matters and a lot of my discussion is based on two books by John Gribbin: *Schrödinger's Cat* (Transworld 1991) and *In Search of SUSY*. (Penguin 1998)

Chapter 6 Reaching for the Self

1. I managed to get back to land but felt myself in a second state for one or two days.

Chapter 9 Choosing the Materials

1. The Noble Eightfold Path is the ten commandments of Buddhism: Right Understanding, Right Thoughts, Right Speech, Right Action, Right Livelihood, Right Effort, Right Mindfulness, Right Concentration.

Chapter 11 The Usefulness of What is Not

1. Law, 1686–1761, was an English Protestant theologian and mystic involved in the rethinking of belief and practice as concerns the Church of England. Influenced himself by Jacob Boehme, he was a great influence on John Wesley, founder of Methodism, and on other reformers.

References

Chapter 1

6 Mikhael Aivanhov, 'Les fruits de l'arbre de vie', p. 271. Fréjus, Editions Prosveta 1996.

Chapter 2

16 *Lao Zi*, chapter 11, Chinese English Bilingual series of Chinese Classics, Hunan Publishing House 1992

19 'The Tibetan Book of the Dead', page xxiv trans. Francesca Fremantle and Chögyam Trungpa. Boston, Shambhala, 1992.

19 Idem page xxv.

21 Koran 50.20-29

21 See 'Kénédougou', by Roland Colin. Paris, Présences africaines, 2004

22 See 'Faith and Reason in Islam, Averroes' Exposition of Religious Arguments', pp. 121-127. Trans. Ibrahim Y. Najjar. Oxford, One World, 2001.

23 See 'Esoteric Buddhism' by A.P. Sinnett, p. 84 London, The Theosophical Publishing Society, 1911.

24 'Treatise on the Resurrection'. See http://www.earlychristianwritings.com

25 The Noble Koran in English Translation by Dr Muhammad Taqi-ud-Din Al Hilali and Dr Muhammad Muhsin Khan, 18.109, King Fahd Complex for the printing of the Holy Koran, Madinah, K.S.A.

27 The New Testament, King James Version. John 9.1-3

Chapter 3

32 See 'Life between Death and Rebirth', Rudolf Steiner, page 135, New York, Anthroposophic Press, 1968.

33 Sri Aurobindo The Life Divine, ch. 19,Lotus Press,2006

36 The Noble Koran in English Translation by Dr Muhammad

Taqi-ud-Din Al Hilali and Dr Muhammad Muhsin Khan, 50.22, 50.19, King Fahd Complex for the printing of the Holy Koran, Madinah, K.S.A.

36 The Upanishads, Breath of the Eternal, page 28, trans. Swami Prabhavananda and Frederick Manchester, New American Library, 1960.

Chapter 4

39 See Roland Colin op. cit.

39 Bhagavad-Gita 15.7, 6.5, 7.24, trans. Juan Mascaro, Penguin Classics, 1961.

41 Bhagavad-Gita 18.20.

42 Fritjof Capra, The Tao of Physics, p. 122, Shambhala, 2000.

Chapter 5

47 The Upanishads, Breath of the Eternal, page 73, trans. Swami Prabhavananda and Frederick Manchester, New American Library, 1960.

49 See 'In Search of SUSY' by John Gribbin, page 117, London, Penguin, 1998.

50 'The Tao of Physics', Fritjof Capra. Boston: Shambhala, 2000.

51 See 'Lao Zi', ch. 35. Chinese-English Bilingual Series of Chinese Classics, Hunan Publishing House, 1992.

Chapter 6

53 See The Perennial Philosophy, Aldous Huxley, page 64, Perennial Classics, Harper Collins, 2004.

54 See 'Faith and Reason in Islam, Averroes' Exposition of Religious Arguments', Trans. Ibrahim Y. Najjar, p. 48, p. 56, Oxford, One World, 2001

55 See Libro de la Vida, Santa Teresa of Avila (translation by author)

56 From the Upanishad Brihadaranyaka. The Upanishads, Breath of the Eternal, trans. Swami Prabhavananda and

Frederick Manchester, New American Library, 1960.
56 The Noble Koran in English Translation by Dr Muhammad Taqi-ud-Din Al Hilali and Dr Muhammad Muhsin Khan, 6.122, King Fahd Complex for the printing of the Holy Koran, Madinah, K.S.A.
57 From the Upanishad Chandogya, The Upanishads, Breath of the Eternal, trans. Swami Prabhavananda and Frederick Manchester, page 78, New American Library, 1960.
57 The New Testament, King James Version.

Chapter 7

62 'The Epic of Gilgamesh', trans. N.K. Sandars. London, Penguin Classics, 1960.
68 The New Testament, King James Version. First Corinthians 15.42-44; 1 Corinthians 13.12
68 See 'Faith and Reason in Islam, Averroes' Exposition of Religious Arguments', p. 121. Trans. Ibrahim Y. Najjar. Oxford, One World, 2001.

Chapter 8

70 The Noble Koran in English Translation by Dr Muhammad Taqi-ud-Din Al Hilali and Dr Muhammad Muhsin Khan, 71, 11.46, 35.35, King Fahd Complex for the printing of the Holy Koran, Madinah, K.S.A.
71 Bible, King James Version, Genesis 6ff.
71 'Teaching of Rumi' Ed. A. Harvey, p. 75, p. 97. Boston, Shambhala, 1999.
72 'Upanishads', trans. Swami Prabhavananda and Frederick Manchester, Chandogya p. 73, NY, Mentor Books, 1957.
72 New Testament, King James Version, Corinthians 1, 12.12
73 See 'Trois Upanishads', Ed. Sri Aurobindo. Paris, Albin Michel, 1972. (Translation by the author)
73 'Upanishads', trans. Swami Prabhavananda and Frederick Manchester, Isha, p. 27, NY, Mentor Books, 1957.

75-76 New Testament, King James Version, Corinthians 1, 15.53, Gospel according to Saint Luke 22.42, 23.34, Gospel according to Saint Matthew, 27.46,

77 Gospel according to Saint John, 16-17, 6.47-50, 17.15-18.

75 'Upanishads', trans. Swami Prabhavananda and Frederick Manchester, Svetasvatara, p. 119, NY, Mentor Books, 1957.

78 Idem, Isha, p. 27.

77 Idem, Chandogya, page p.78.

78 Idem, Isha, p. 28.

79 'The Buddha and His Teaching', by Narada Maha Thera, p. 279. Colombo 1964.

80 'Esoteric Buddhism', A.P. Sinnett, p. 82. London, Theosophical Publishing Society, 1911.

81 Koran 71

82 'Upanishads', trans. Swami Prabhavananda and Frederick Manchester, Mundaka, p. 47, NY, Mentor Books, 1957.

Chapter 9

83 'Upanishads', trans. Swami Prabhavananda and Frederick Manchester, Mundaka, p 47, NY, Mentor Books, 1957.

83 The Noble Koran in English Translation by Dr Muhammad Taqi-ud-Din Al Hilali and Dr Muhammad Muhsin Khan, 18.54ff, 45.15, King Fahd Complex for the printing of the Holy Koran, Madinah, K.S.A.

84 'The Dhammapada', Narada Maha Thera, Kuala Lumpur, BMS 1978.

85 'A Manual of Abhidhamma', by Narada Maha Thera, p. 65. Kuala Lumpur, BMS, 1956.

86 On thoughts processes in Buddhism see Narada, 'The Buddha and His Teachings', ch. 20, Buddhist Missionary Society, Colombo, 1964.

87 idem 449.

Chapter 10

90 Saint Teresa of Avila: Libro de la Vida, Salamanca 1588, translations by the author.

91 Saint John of the Cross: Poems, trans. Roy Campbell. London, Penguin Classics 1960.

92 'Upanishads', trans. Swami Prabhavananda and Frederick Manchester, Svetasvatara and Brihadaranyaka, NY, Mentor Books, 1957.

94 'Teaching of Rumi' Ed. A. Harvey, p.35, 65, 132. Boston, Shambhala, 1999.

97 'The Buddha and His Teachings', Narada,see above ch. 8.

98 'La Vie divine' by Sri Aurobindo, ch. 23. Paris, Albin Michel, 1973. (Translation by the author)

99 'Life after Death', by Deepak Chopra, ch. 9. NY: Harmony Books, 2006.

99 Bible, King James Version, Psalms 82.6

100 'Upanishads', trans. Swami Prabhavananda and Frederick Manchester, Isha, NY, Mentor Books, 1957.

100 'Anthroposophie et les forces du coeur humain', lectures Sept-Oct. 1923, Vienna, published in German as 'Die Antroposophie und das menschliche Gemüt' (Rudolf Steiner Verlag, Dornach, Switzerland). Paris: Triades 1976.

102 'Upanishads', trans. Swami Prabhavananda and Frederick Manchester, Kaivalya, NY, Mentor Books, 1957.

Chapter 11

105 'Lao Zi', Chinese-English Bilingual Series of Chinese Classics, Hunan Publishing House, 1992.

113 'The Book of Change', Anon. Trans. Wang Rangpei, Ren Xiuhua. Shanghai Foreign Language Education Press, 1993.

111 See 'Trois Upanishads', Ed. Sri Aurobindo. Paris, Albin Michel, 1972. (Translation by the author)

114 Bhagavad-Gita 3.16, 3.17, trans. Juan Mascaro, Penguin Classics, 1961.

115 'The Perennial Philosophy', Aldous Huxley. NY: Perennial Classics, 2004.
116 Bhagavad-Gita 9.27, 12.10, trans. Juan Mascaro, Penguin Classics, 1961.
117 For the term 'Inner Light' see Lao Zi ch. 52.

Chapter 12

121 The Gospel of Saint Thomas, trans. Steven Patterson and Marvin Meyer, HYPERLINK http://www.earlycrhistain/ http://www.earlychristianwritings.com
121 English and Scottish Ballads, Ed. Robert Graves, Heinemann 1957
122 Bible King James Version, First Epistle of Saint John 3.
122 The Noble Koran in English Translation by Dr Muhammad Taqi-ud-Din Al Hilali and Dr Muhammad Muhsin Khan, 2.165, King Fahd Complex for the printing of the Holy Koran, Madinah, K.S.A.
122 'The Cosmogony of the Rosicrucians', Max Heindel. Fellowship of the Rosicrucian Society 1922.
124 Also sprach Zarathustra, F. Nietzsche, 'On love of one's neighbour', 1885.
124 New Testament, King James Version, First Corinthians13
125 'Upanishads', trans. Swami Prabhavananda and Frederick Manchester, Isha, NY, Mentor Books, 1957.
132 Bhagavad-Gita 6.30, 2.11, 18.11, 9.27-31trans. Juan Mascaro, Penguin Classics, 1961
135 'Upanishads', trans. Swami Prabhavananda and Frederick Manchester, Kena, NY, Mentor Books, 1957.

Chapter 13

139 See Steiner archive on Lucifer and Ahriman. http://www.rsarchive.org
140 Max Heindel op.cit. see above ch. 12.
141 Bible, King James Version, Book of Genesis 1.1.

142 'Antroposophie et les forces du coeur humain', lectures Sept-Oct. 1923, Vienna, published in German as 'Die Antroposophie und das menschliche Gemüt' (Rudolf Steiner Verlag, Dornach, Switzerland). Paris: Triades 1976.
144 'Chaos', James Gleik. London: Minerva, 1988.
144 'The Tao of Physics', Fritjof Capra, p. 137. Boston: Shambhala, 2000.
145 in his commentaries on Three Upanishads, see above chapter 11.

Chapter 14

148 'Les Mystères de Iesod', Mikhael Aivanhov, p. 223. Fréjus, Oeuvres Complètes Tome VII, 1973. Translation by the author.
148 Bhagavad-Gita 15.12, trans. Juan Mascaro, Penguin Classics, 1961.
150 Bhagavad Gita 16.9, trans. Juan Mascaro, Penguin Classics, 1961.
152 'Upanishads', trans. Swami Prabhavananda and Frederick Manchester, Brihadaranyaka, NY, Mentor Books, 1957.
157 Bhagavad-Gita 2.63, trans. Juan Mascaro, Penguin Classics
157 Jalal-Udin Rumi, in 'Teaching of Rumi' Ed. A. Harvey, p. 142. Boston, Shambhala, 1999.
158 'La forces des choses' Simone de Beauvoir. Edition??

Chapter 15

160 The Power of Now, Eckhart Tolle, Novatoca, New World Library 1999
163 'Life after Death', by Deepak Chopra, ch. 9. NY: Harmony Books, 2006.
164 Saint John of the Cross: Poems, trans. Roy Campbell. London, Penguin Classics 1960.
164 'Pensées', Blaise Pascal, number 712 trans. J.M. Cohen. Penguin Classics, 1961.

165 'Upanishads', Brihadaranyaka, Aitareya, Prasna, trans. Swami Prabhavananda and Frederick Manchester, Brihadaranyaka, NY, Mentor Books, 1957.
165 Bhagavad-Gita 6.18-19, 15.7, trans. Juan Mascaro, Penguin Classics
165 'The Hidden Teaching Beyond Yoga', Paul Brunton, p. 293. Century Paperbacks, 1982.
168 The Noble Koran in English Translation by Dr Muhammad Taqi-ud-Din Al Hilali and Dr Muhammad Muhsin Khan, 3.37, King Fahd Complex for the printing of the Holy Koran, Madinah, K.S.A.
169 'Upanishads', Svetasvatara, trans. Swami Prabhavananda and Frederick Manchester, Brihadaranyaka, NY, Mentor Books, 1957.

Chapter 16

173 Bhagavad-Gita 2.19, trans. Juan Mascaro, Penguin Classics.
176 'The Other Side', James Pike. New Focus Foundation, 1968.
177 'Esoteric Buddhism' by A.P. Sinnett, pp. 122-130, London, The Theosophical Publishing Society, 1911.
184 Steiner 'Life between Death and Rebirth' p. 170 and p. 167.
181 'Les fruits de l'arbre de vie', Mikhael Aivanhov, p. 210-211. Fréjus, Prosveta: Oeuvres Complètes Tome 32, 1987., (Author's translation)
182 Steiner, R : 'Life between Death and Rebirth' pp. 24-25, New York, Anthroposophic Press, 1968.

BOOKS

O is a symbol of the world, of oneness and unity. In different cultures it also means the "eye," symbolizing knowledge and insight. We aim to publish books that are accessible, constructive and that challenge accepted opinion, both that of academia and the "moral majority."

Our books are available in all good English language bookstores worldwide. If you don't see the book on the shelves ask the bookstore to order it for you, quoting the ISBN number and title. Alternatively you can order online (all major online retail sites carry our titles) or contact the distributor in the relevant country, listed on the copyright page.

See our website **www.o-books.net** for a full list of over 500 titles, growing by 100 a year.

And tune in to myspiritradio.com for our book review radio show, hosted by June-Elleni Laine, where you can listen to the authors discussing their books.

MySpiritRadio